A Beginner's Guide to Options Trading

Learn to Open an Options Trading Account, Become an Option Trader, Know the Strategies, and Make a Huge Income from Your Investments

By

Benjamin T. Buffett

© Copyright 2020 by Benjamin T. Buffett

All rights reserved.

This document is geared towards providing exact and reliable information in regards to the topic and issue covered. The publication is sold with the idea that the publisher is not required to render accounting, officially permitted, or otherwise qualified services. If advice is necessary, legal or professional, a practiced individual in the profession should be ordered.

- From a Declaration of Principles which was accepted and approved equally by a Committee of the American Bar Association and a Committee of Publishers and Associations.

In no way is it legal to reproduce, duplicate, or transmit any part of this document in either electronic means or printed format. Recording of this publication is strictly prohibited, and any storage of this document is not allowed unless with written permission from the publisher. All rights reserved.

The information provided herein is stated to be truthful and consistent, in that any liability, in terms of inattention or otherwise, by any usage or abuse of any policies, processes, or directions contained within is the solitary and utter responsibility of the recipient reader. Under no circumstances will any legal responsibility or blame be held against the publisher for any reparation, damages, or monetary loss due to the information herein, either directly or indirectly.

Respective authors own all copyrights not held by the publisher.

The information herein is offered for informational purposes solely and is universal as so. The presentation of the information is without a contract or any guarantee assurance.

The trademarks that are used are without any consent, and the publication of the trademark is without permission or backing by the trademark owner. All trademarks and brands within this book are for clarifying purposes only and are owned by the owners themselves, not affiliated with this document.

TABLE OF CONTENTS

INTRODUCTION 4

CHAPTER 1: INTRODUCTION TO OPTIONS TRADING 5
- DEFINING OPTIONS TRADING 9
- HISTORY OF OPTIONS TRADING 15
- 1.3. REASONS TO TRADE OPTIONS 21

CHAPTER 2: OPENING AN OPTIONS TRADING ACCOUNT 34
- 2.1. HOW TO START AN OPTIONS TRADING ACCOUNT? 34
- 2.2. WHAT KIND OF ACCOUNT SHOULD BE OPENED TO BEGIN OPTION TRADING? 43
- 2.3. CORE ELEMENTS IN OPTIONS TRADING 53
- 2.4. BEST OPTIONS TRADING PLATFORMS 58

CHAPTER 3: OPTION TRADING STRATEGIES 66
- 3.1 OPTIONS TRADING STRATEGIES 72
- 3.2. TIPS FOR EFFECTIVE USE OF OPTIONS TRADING STRATEGIES 91

CHAPTER 4: BECOME A GOOD OPTIONS TRADER 106
- 4.1 BEST WAYS TO MASTER THE OPTIONS TRADING.. 106
- 4.2 TIPS TO BECOME A PRO OPTIONS TRADER 115

CHAPTER 5: MAKE A HUGE INCOME FROM INVESTING IN OPTIONS TRADING AND OTHER ASSETS 119
- 5.1 10 STEPS TO SUCCESSFUL INCOME INVESTING FOR BEGINNERS 119
- 5.2. 10 OPTIONS TRADING MISTAKES TO AVOID 132
- 5.3. HOW TO MAKE YOUR INVESTMENTS GROW 138
- 5.4. PICK RIGHT OPTION TO TRADE IN SIX STEPS 142

CONCLUSION 152

INTRODUCTION

Trading options is a way to leverage assets for savvy investors and manage some of the risks associated with playing the market. Nearly every investor knows the saying "Buy low and sell high". But with options, it's possible to benefit when stocks go up, down or sideways. With a relatively small cash outlay, you can use the options to cut losses, protect profits and monitor large chunks of stock.

On the other side, tactics for the options can be difficult and dangerous. Not only you could lose your entire investment, you may also be exposed to theoretically unlimited losses by some strategies.

CHAPTER 1: INTRODUCTION TO OPTIONS TRADING

Options are financial instruments, the value of which is extracted from the value of an underlying (aka involved) asset such as security or estate. An option deal provides the buyer with the opportunity to buy or sell, depending on one's view of the value of the security involved. Holding a call option gives the right to buy shares at the strike price on expiration, and owning a put option gives the right to sell at expiry at the strike price.

The options do not always need to be exercised at the expiry and the strike price when acquired or sold. They can be exercised at any time until the option expires. So, if the options are used wisely, they are considered less risky than stocks or futures contracts. As a consequence of this scheme, options are considered derivative instruments-meaning that their price is derived from the assets involved. Options, however, do not reflect ownership in the business.

Why would an investor exploit options?

When an investor or trader purchases a contract for calls, he/she places bets on the stock price to go in his / her favour (up for call option and down for pit option).

The price at which one agrees to buy the asset in question through the option is called the "strike price," and the price paid for getting this right is called the "options bonus."

Contract Options Benefits

Here are some of key profits of contracts with Options:

The Options contract, as the name suggests, offers the option buyer the right to exercise his choice if he wishes. If the Spot price does not go in favour of the contract buyer, he does not have to exercise his right, and then he will lose only the premium.

One-time premium is the only cost that option buyer has to pay to be a part of a bigger game and ride the momentum of the underlying price.

If an option seller has the opposite view of an option buyer, he can only sell the contract option and the premium profit from the wallet.

The options are less risky compared to equities. For instance, if a trader wants to buy 1000 Reliance shares, then at CMP (PRs 1400 per share), P.R.s 14, 00,000 (fourteen lakhs) has to be shed out. But by purchasing contracts with two call options (500 shares each), one can express the same opinion. Tell if he buys by paying a premium of 35 per share, at the 1410 CE Money deal. Therefore, the total cost would be only P.R.s. 35000 = (500 * 35 * 2).

So, now, if the opportunity for option buyer was expired Out of Cash, he's just standing to lose the premium. But, if Reliance Industries' share price goes down to P.R.s. 1300, then gross equity shareholders loss would be P.R.s. 1,00,000 (1000*100).

Return on investment is very good for an option buyer because the cost paid is only the premium, and the potential return is infinite.

Options Call and Place

Call/Put options are financial derivative instruments, meaning their movement depends on the movement of the asset or security involved in the bid. The main purpose of buying a call option is for the trader/investor to expect the price of the security involved to go up in the near future, and vice versa for the seller of the call option.

The trader or investor purchases a Put option when he expects the price of an asset involved to decline in the near future and vice versa for seller or writer of the contract. Although the option writer receives premium when selling, it runs the risk of giving up the asset involved if the options are in favour of the buyer option.

For U.S. type options, a sales contract call option allows the purchaser to acquire the resource at the strike price at any time before the contract expiry date.

In the case of an option in European format, the owner of the call has the power to only exercise on the expiry date.

If the spot price moves above the strike price before expiry and call option writer to bind by his word, it is advantageous for the call buyer to allow his right to sell his call option.

The premium charged by the option holder gives him the right to purchase the stock or security in question at the strike price before the options agreement expires. If the asset's price goes above the strike price, then the option is in the money.

Author options get the premium. The premium earned is a way for the choice writer or seller to earn revenue. But the income of the option writer is limited to the money received as a premium and runs the infinite risk of paying up the option buyer in case the protection involved goes above the price of the strike.

Call choices can be in, at, or Money-Out. For e.g., if the Index is currently trading at 9500, an In the Money Call option will be buying the option with the strike below 9500 (say 9400 CE), An At the Money Call option will be buying an option will be the strike price at 9500 and an Out of Money Call option will be to the strike price above 9500 (say 9600 CE). The In-the-money call option is the most expensive one, and the out-of-money options are the cheapest, but they bear the greatest chance of useless expiry.

Dismantle Placed Options

The length of the contract options can vary from very short-term (weekly) to long -term(monthly) contracts. If the spot price of the security involved falls below the strike price, it is advantageous for the put option buyer to exercise or sell his choice.

The premium paid by the put option buyer gives him the right to sell the stock or security in dispute at the strike price before the options agreement expires.

And Put options can be in or Out of the money just like a Call option. For example, if the Index is currently trading at 9500, an In the Money Placed option will be to purchase the option with the strike above 9500 (say 9600 PE), An At the Money Put option will be to purchase the strike price at 9500, and an Out of Money Put option will be to but strike price below 9500 (say 9400 PE).

DEFINING OPTIONS TRADING

Options are contracts where a seller gives a buyer the right, but not the duty, to purchase or sell a specified number of shares at a predetermined price within a specified time limit.

Options are derivatives, meaning that their value comes from an underlying investment.

Quite often, the underlying investment on which an option is based is the shareholdings in a publicly-traded firm. Many underlying investments which may be based on options include equity indices, Exchange Traded Funds (ETFs), government securities, foreign currencies, or commodities such as agricultural or industrial products. Contracts on stock options are for 100 percent of the underlying stock-an exception will be when changes are made for stock splits or mergers.

Options are exchanged among institutional investors, individual investors, and skilled traders on the securities market places and it can be for one contract or many.

An option contract is specified by the following elements: form (Put or Call), underlying security, trade unit (share number), strike price and expiry date. All option contracts of the same nature, design and cover the same concealed security are indicated as a class of options. All options of the same class that also have the same unit of exchange at the same price and expiry date of the strike are referred to as a series of options.

Tools Words and Concepts

First of all, becoming conversant requires learning some key terms. Here are the basics for beginning investors to trade options.

Definitions for contract options

On contract options, there are four key important things to know:

1. Option types: There are two types of options which can be purchased or sold:

Call: An options contract that delivers you the right to purchase stock at a fixed price within a certain period of time.

Put: A contract of options that gives you the right to sell stock at a fixed price within a given period of time.

2. Day of expiration: Date on which contract options becomes void. It is your due date to do something with the contract, and in the future, it can be days, weeks, months, or years.

3. The strike price, or exercise price: The price at which if you choose to exercise the option, you will buy or sell the stock.

4. Premium: The price you pay per share for an option. The prime is made up of:

Intrinsic value: The value of an option established on the difference between the actual market price of a stock and the strike price of the option.

Time value: The value of an option established on time before the expiry of the contract. Time is valuable to investors as it is likely that the intrinsic value of an option will increase during the time frame of the contract. Time value decreases as the expiration date approaches. This is called time decay or "theta," after the model of pricing options used to quantify it.

Comments on the stock option clarified.

Call a stock quote, and you get the company's current market share price — the amount you would pay if you purchased them, or the amount you would earn if you sold them. Contract quotes for options are much more complicated because there are multiple versions available for trade based on type, expiry date, strike price, and more.

Strike: The price you would be paying or getting if you exercised the option.

Option Name: Just as stocks have ticker symbols, contract options have option symbols with letters and numbers that suit the specifics in a contract. In a real chain of options, the firm's ticker symbol will come before the name of the deal.

Last: The amount that was paid last time the option was exchanged or earned.

Bid: The amount a purchaser wishes to pay for the option. If you offer an option, this is the price you will get for the deal.

Ask: The price a seller will consider for the option. If you want to buy an option that is the price you will pay.

Change: The price change since the close of the previous trading day, also expressed in percentage terms.

Volume: The number of traded contracts that specific day.

Open interest: The number of contracts currently in play with options.

Volatility: A measure of the amount to which a stock price fluctuates between the high and low price each day. As the name implies, historical volatility is determined using preceding price data. It can be measured annually or within a given time frame.

Implied volatility, or "IV" in shorthand options-quote, tests how likely the market thinks a stock will undergo a price change. (You might also hear of "Vega," the market model option that is used to calculate the theoretical impact on the implied volatility of each one-point change in stock price.)

Higher implied volatility usually implies higher prices for options due to the higher possible contract upside. But don't take those estimates as guarantees. Just as earnings estimates are merely the forecast by an analyst of what a firm is likely to earn, volatility indicators are only predictions of how much the price of an option can change.

Terms defining what a choice might be worth

Not cutting it when it comes to describing output choices, saying "up," "down," or "flat." It is one of three things at any given moment when an options contract is in play:

In the money: This applies to an option that has intrinsic value — when the relationship between the open market stock price and the strike price benefits the contract owner's options. If the selling price is higher than the strike price, then that is good news for the call option holders. If the purchase price is lower than the strike price, then a put option is in the bank.

Out of the money: It's called out of the money when there's no financial advantage to using the right. In practical terms, an out-of-the-money option makes it less profitable to buy or sell stock at the strike price than to buy or sell on the open market. If the stock price is lower than the strike price, then a call option is out of pocket. A put option can be considered out of the market, when the stock price is higher than the strike price.

At the money: If the value of the stock is approximately equal to the price of the strike, an option is considered at the money. It is essentially a wash-up.

Purchaser and seller options

These two types include options traders. This is an additional example in which common terms such as "buyer" and "seller" do not quite reflect the complexities of trading options.

Holder: This refers to the investor who owns a contract for the options. A call holder might pay for the option of purchasing that stock based on contract parameters. A put holder shall have all the right to sell that stock.

Writer: A reference to the investor selling the contract options. In exchange to sell or buy the specified securities at the strike price. In addition to being on other side of the transaction, their revelation to risk is the biggest difference between options writers and option holders.

History of Options Trading

Trading options are a relatively like new method of investing as compared with other traditional forms like purchasing shares and stocks. The current options agreements as we know that were only implemented when the (Chicago Board of Options Exchange) CBOE was created, but it is believed that the basic understanding of options contracts was developed in Ancient Greece: perhaps in the mid-fourth century B.C.

Since then, options have been around us in one method or another in the diverse marketplaces, since the establishment of the CBOE in 1973, when they were fully regulated for the very first time, and there has been some interest in trading options. We provide details about the history of trading options, beginning with Ancient Greece and going through forward to modern-day age.

- Thales and the Variety of Olives
- 17th Century Tulip Mania
- Bans on Trading Options
- Russell Sage and the Call and Place Brokers
- The Options Market Listed

Thales and the Variety of Olives

Thales was very interested in mathematics and astronomy, among other topics, and he joint his understanding of those subjects to establish what probably was the first known contract of options. By observing the stars, Thales, likely managed to predict that his region would have a large olive harvest and set out to take advantage of his prediction. He recognised that there would be considerable demand for olive presses and basically wanted to corner the market.

Thales, however, did not have enough funds to own all the olive presses; so instead, he paid a sum of money to each of the owners of olive presses to secure the right to use them at harvest time. When harvest time came and, as Thales had predicted, it was indeed an enormous harvest, Thales resold rights to olive presses to those who always wanted them with a substantial profit.

17th Century Tulip Bulb Mania

Another important incident in options history was an event in Holland in the 17th century that is extensively denoted to as Tulip Bulb Mania. Tulips were extremely popular in the region at the time and were considered Dutch aristocracy to be status symbols. Their influence spread across Europe and the world, and this led to a drastic increase in demand for tulip bulbs.

The demand for tulip bulbs continued to rise during the 1630s, and, as a result, the price also grew in value. As a result, the worth of tulip bulb options contracts has increased, and a (secondary) market emerged for those contracts that allowed anyone to gamble on the tulip bulb market. In Holland, many families or some individuals invested heavily contracts, often using all their capital they had, or even borrowing assets like houses or some property.

Tulip bulbs kept rising on price, but could only go on for so long, and finally, the bubble busted.

Prices had grown to the point where they were unenforceable, and as prices began to fall, consumers began to disappear. Many of those who bet everything on the rising price of continued growing tulip bulbs have been entirely wiped out. People lost their entire money and their homes. The Netherlands economy has fallen into recession.

Since the options market was unregulated, and there was no other way to compel investors to meet their options contract obligations options gained a bad name all over the world.

Bans on Trading Options

This was mostly due to the fact they provided great leverage capacity, which in fact, is one of the main reasons that why so famous today. So, trading of these contracts continued, but they couldn't do anything to their bad or poor reputation. There was increasing resistance to their use.

Over the course of history, alternatives in many parts of the world have been banned numerous times: mostly in Europe, USA and Japan. The most distinguished bans may have been in London (England). This ban continued for more than Hundred years and was not lifted until later in the 19th century.

Russell Sage and the Call and Place Brokers

A significant development in options trading history has involved an American's financier named Russell Sage. Sage began creating calls in the 19th century and puts options that traded over the offset in the USA. Still no formal barter market, but Sage created an activity that was a major breakthrough for trading options.

Sage is also thought to be the first person who found a price relationship between an option price, the underlying interest rates and security price. He used to put-call parity to formulate synthetic loans generated by him buying stock and a related put from a client.

Sage eventually stopped trading due to significant losses in his path, but he was definitely instrumental in the evolution of trading options. There was definitely a rise in options trading by this stage, although the lack of any oversight meant investors were still wary.

The Options Market Listed

The options market continued to be controlled essentially by putting and calling brokers. There has been some industry standardisation, and more people have become aware of all these potential uses and contracts. The market at this time remained relatively illiquid with limited or small activity.

Although the U.S. (Securities and Exchange Commission) SEC had bought some oversight into the over-the-counter options market, their trading did not actually advance at any significant pace by the late 1960s. There were too many complexities involved, and volatile rates made serious consideration of options as a viable tradable instrument quite difficult for any investor.

In 1968 it was an entirely unrelated event that ultimately led to a solution that would ultimately bring the options market into the mainstream.

There were several hurdles to overcome for this to become feasible, but the Chicago Options Exchange Board (CBOE) started trading in 1973. For the first time, contract options were fully regulated, and they had to be traded on a fair marketplace. At the same time, the Options Clearing Company was set up for centralised clearing and ensuring that contracts are properly fulfilled. Thus, eliminating many of the investors' fears regarding un-honoured contracts still held. Over 2,000 years after Thales produced the first call, it was finally legal to sell options.

1.3. REASONS TO TRADE OPTIONS

Benefits of Trading Options

The reason why so many investors appeal to buy stocks or trade them is because it's relatively easy to do, and there is certainly money to make. Often the trading of other financial tools is more difficult, and this is possibly why many traders and investors prefer to stay with stocks. Some of these other financial instruments, however, will offer other advantages that stocks don't.

In particular, options trading has many rewards, and there are so many of reasons why this method of trading is worth to consider for those who are looking to invest. This addresses the following topics:

- An outlay of capital and cost-efficiency
- Risk and Reward
- Odds for Trading Options

Capital outlay & cost-effectiveness

One of the outclass reasons for trading options is that, without necessarily having to have large sums of money, it is possible to make significant profits from doing so.

Let's say you had $2,000 to spend, for example, and you decided to invest it in Company XY stock, which is currently trading at $30, which you expected to increase in value. If you actually use your $2,000 to buy those stocks, then you could buy 51 shares. If the stock rose to, say, $24, then for a total of $24, you'd make a profit of $4 per share. It represents a return on your original investment of 24 percent.

This makes it ideal for investors with little starting capital and those with larger budgets. The potential for large profits from small investments is largely down to leverage use. You can use the leverage in very simple terms to get more trading power from the money you own.

Alternatively, you could purchase call options on the same stock, granting you the right to buy the stock. If call options were selling at $3 each with a strike price of $30, you could buy 600 options, which would allow you to buy 600 shares if the stock went up. With the stock growing to $26, you may exercise your option to buy 600 shares, and then immediately sell them for $2,600 in profit.

After taking away your initial $1,000 investment to purchase the options, you still have a profit of $1,500 and a return of 150 percent on your assets. This is a somehow clear example, but it does demonstrate how, from whatever starting resources you have at your fingertips, you can generate significant returns.

Very simply, when you take a particular position on the related underlying security, you can save money, which allows you to make very cost-efficient investments and trades. There are even a number of strategies that can be directly used to lower the cost of taking certain positions.

Reward and Risk

The extensive range of different options contracts you can trade with and the dissimilar orders you can place makes it much easier to limit that risk than when you simply buy and sell stocks. When you know more about options and how they are traded, you can understand how important an instrument can be when it comes to risk management.

It would be clear that, there are risks involved as there is any type of investment. Certain trading strategies, can be indeed very risky. The general rule is that the higher the possible return, the greater the risk level involved. Nevertheless, what is especially great is the fact that you can choose pretty much whatever risk you wish to take and trade them accordingly.

Odds for Trading Options

It is easy to observe why many investors are becoming more and more familiar with trading options.

It's no longer just the experts involved, as the incentives on offer are taking advantage of more and more home traders and casual investors. Yet it's not without its inconveniences.

It's not a simple task to master options trading, and there's certainly a lot to gain and learn. That is probably the biggest reason why so many are still avoiding it, as the subject's complexities may seem daunting or even intimidating. Because it's just not as simple as many other forms of investment is certainly a major drawback. There's gain to be made. But we are learning how it takes a lot of time and effort. The risks involved are yet another disadvantage. While there are risks in any investment form, trading options can be risky, especially for the beginners who don't have an enormous amount of experience. If you understand the strategies, they can be used to limit risk, but this form of trading should not be considered risk-free in any way.

Four key reasons investors use portfolio options

Investors use options strategies in their portfolios for four main reasons: versatility, leverage, hedging, and generation of profits.

1. Flexible

When buying stock, your gain depends solely on the price that goes up.

But if a stock rises – or if it falls – options can provide potential benefits. That means you can guess about a stock's future price, whether it is going up or not.

2. Leverage

Leverage means that you can use less money to expose yourself to the movement of the price of a stock. In other words, you are gaining market exposure with options that are close to buying a stock, but basically, you are spending less money to make it happen, and that might mean more flexibility for both you and your portfolio.

3. Deposit

Hedging is about Risk Management. You make trades situated on your best judgment, and options will help protect those trades — or your overall portfolio — in the event that things don't work as you intended to.

4. Revenue generation

One of the biggest reasons some investors are trading options is revenue generation. Like a dividend on stock, options can be used to help create a stream of revenue. There are strategies for options that allow you to collect money on your existing or future stock positions.

One of the main reasons some investors are trading options is revenue generation. Unlike a dividend on stock, options can be used to help build a source of revenue. There are strategies for options that allow you to earn money either on your current or future stock positions.

In the most common types of accounts, you can trade options, including your brokerage account, certain types of retirement accounts, and even you're IRA. Do not forget about these four big reasons people use options the next time you're thinking about trading stocks.

Why Use Trade Option?

Why do you really need to learn to trade options? Why options for trade?

What exactly can one learn about this financial instrument from putting in time and energy?

Why trade options? After so many decimvir of development along with centuries of life, today options trading remains one of the world's most mysterious and misunderstood form of investing. Options are one of the most effective financial instruments ever made, but they are also one of the most complicated, and with the many entry barriers as well as difficulties to overcome in order even to open a trading account options, people often ask themselves why they should even bother learning about trading options when there are simpler ways of investing like stocks. The guide will try to explain some explanations about why options are something every experienced investor and trader should learn and use.

Options Trading Reason 1: Do More with Less!

Leverage is the option. Leverage means you can do the same with less capital, or even more with less money than with conventional means of investment. Leverage is expressed in trading options allowing you to trade in stocks using only a small fraction of their price! For example, at the time of writing, AAPL (Apple Inc.) stocks are trading at $101.87. You would need $101.87 x 100 = $10,187 to buy 100 shares of AAPL stocks. However, you can trade the profits on AAPL's 100 shares simply by purchasing its $101 strike price call options for just $2.30 per contract, which is just $2.30 x 100 = $230! Yes, you can control AAPL's 100-share profits if it rises at just $230 if you traded its options for $10,187 instead of its stocks! It makes trading options a perfect alternative for traders with very little capital to invest with but wants to be interested in the movements of these great companies. Such leverage also allows traders with just very little money to begin with making meaningful amounts of profit through this option leverage effect.

Trading options Reason 2: Take less risk than stocks!

Contrary to popular belief, trading options may, in fact, be less risky than trading the same stock! Too much abuse of options leading to catastrophic losses and wipeouts of accounts has been popularised by the media to the point that most people think trading options is extremely risky. Indeed, this belief is so widespread that it has become increasingly difficult over the past few decades to open an options trading account, as regulators also believe that options are riskier than stocks. How can options be less risky than stocks? By the fact that you risk nothing more than the money that you use to buy the options! Sure, take our example of 100 shares in AAPL stocks above. As a stock trader, you lose the entire $10,187 in trading while the options trader just lost $230 (and no more!) in trading the same 100 shares! If AAPL drops from $101.87 to $91.68 by 10 percent, the stock trader will lose $1,018.70 while the options trader will lose only $230 no matter how low AAPL goes to, even $0!

Selling Options Reason 3: More Ways to Win Than Trading Bonds!

If you trade stocks, i.e., if you buy stocks, you just win when the stock goes up. There is no other way to win as you do nothing when the stock has not moved, and when the stock goes down, you make a loss.

However, that's not the case with options trading. In fact, you could win in more than one direction at the same time by using options strategies! For e.g., you could win if the stock stagnates or moves in one direction, you could win if the stock goes either up or down in either direction, and you could also win if the stock stagnates, moves up a bit or down a little, in all three directions! How's that able to increase your winning chances? The imaginative use of these options strategies is the real magic behind options trading, which makes a financial alchemy a few trading options.

Trading options Reason 4: It's Math Fun for Geeks!

Oh yeah, if you're a math nerd or a quant geek, you'd be absolutely blown away by what you can do when you're applying complex mathematical calculations to options role building. In fact, you could create options positions with the correct calculations and formula that do absolutely everything, exactly how you want it! When you start creating your own payoff profile calculators or trade calculators, the real magic of options strategies is released to mathematically arrive at the exact composition of options for the exact payoff and reward risk profile you're trying to create. In addition, you could also construct algorithms mathematically to leverage the many arbitrage possibilities offered by an instrument as complex as options. Yeah, anyone of the many Greek options can be used for benefit! For Geeks, choices are Greeks too!

Reason 5 Trading Options: It is Easy!

Before that last reason makes you think options are too hard for ordinary people to learn, the fact is that it can be very simple! Yes, the options' beauty is that they can be as complex or as simple as you want them to be! Moving into the world of quantum mathematics can be complicated enough, but it can also be as easy as opening an options trading account with renowned options brokers like Optionsxpress.com and then buying when the stock goes up and selling when the stock goes down! Indeed, at its heart, trading options are as simple as buying call options on stocks that you think will go up and purchasing stock options that you think will go down in order to benefit (akin to short a stock). It's so easy!

Reason 6 Trading Options: Works with Stocks!

Yeah, if you're a stock trader, you'll need to learn more about trading options to further your stock income and secure your stock holdings as well! Options are not only financial instruments that you can sell on your own, but also something that you can use for your portfolio holdings as steroids or insurance! If you want to cover your stocks from dropping in value when their price drops, just buy the options for protecting those stocks: this is called Defensive Placed. If you want to benefit from stable and not moving stocks, simply sell them out of the money call options and receive "rent money" safely!

This is called Covered Call! Cover your stocks and steroids! Is there any reason why stock traders shouldn't know how to trade options?

Reason 7 Trading Options: Choose your own level of risk!

One great thing about options that make it better than futures (in this aspect) is that unlike fixed futures trading leverage that fixes the level of risk you 're playing at, you can actually choose your own level of risk while trading options. This means that options can be as dangerous or as safe as you would like them to be! If you gamble with money, you can afford to lose lottery style, and you could choose to trade options with an extremely high level of leverage, which returns hundreds of dollars of benefit when the underlying stock moves strongly but risks losing the entire amount of money that was put into that trade if the stock did not work that way. For example, if you feel greedy on AAPL and trade with money that you can afford to lose, you might want to buy it out of the money call options for maybe only $0.50 per contract, working out just $50 to manage 100 AAPL shares (now who can't afford to lose $50?).

Buying this option could mean a return of 1000 percent if AAPL's price rises by 10 percent, but it only means you 're losing your entire investment of $50 if AAPL failed to move that much.

On the other hand, if you feel more conservative and want to reduce the percentage loss if AAPL fails to move or actually decreases, you can choose options that are at the money or in the money using the same amount of money so that if AAPL fails to move that strongly, you may lose 40 percent or 50 percent instead of 100 percent of that money. So, you can adapt the level of risk you want to engage in options trading! With the huge number of options available for contracts for each optional stock, there is definitely an option or combination of options that match your specific risk appetite. This is something that you are not going to get in futures trading or stock trading.

Trading options Reason 8: Options Forgive Mistakes!

When you make a mistake in trading stocks, all you can do is just watch helplessly as the stock's value goes down with no means of intervention to stop the loss or even reverse the loss. That is not the case with trading options, though! You might actually transform the options position creatively when you make a mistake with options in order to stop the position from making any further losses and even reverse the loss so that it starts recovering into a profit! In reality, using options too, you could even fix losing stock positions. Yeah, that's why options are so fun, it gives you the ability to take advantage of any situation and convert it into your advantage as long as you are imaginative and adequately familiar with the almost unlimited ways of writing positions.

No more holding and waiting, options give you the power to take into your own hands the fate and outcome of your trading account in any and all market conditions!

Trading options Explanation 9: Options are highly liquid!

Options are so highly liquid in the U.S. market and European markets that you can trade options even if you have a very large fund. A lot of beginners are often concerned with whether options are sufficiently liquid to trade with significant fund size, and the simple answer is yes, options are liquid enough to trade large fund sizes with. As such, if what stops you from trading options is that you believe your fund size is too big for it, then rest assured that today's options market is large enough and liquid enough for very large fund sizes. However, with that being said, contracts of options will always exist, which may not be as liquid as you need to be. As such, as options traders, we need to know how to tell if a contract option is sufficiently liquid for our size of the trade, and simply avoid those that are not.

CHAPTER 2: OPENING AN OPTIONS TRADING ACCOUNT

An option is a contract that states you have the right to purchase or sell an asset at any time before a certain date at a certain price, but you are not forced to do so. Options are split into 'call' and 'put' with a call option; you have the right to buy an asset before a given data at a certain price.

2.1. How to Start an Options Trading Account?

If you had expected the value of the asset to rise before that date, you should buy this option, so you could buy it cheaper. The opposite is a Put alternative. You buy the right to sell an asset, which would be useful if you thought that the price of that asset would drop before a date. That is the basic trading options procedure, though it is very complex and extremely risky in operation. If you are interested in this high-risk investment, make sure you take the time to educate yourself and invest only with venture capital.

Part 1 Comprising the Options

Know what kind of options it provides. Options are contracts that grant their holder the right to buy or sell an underlying security at a fixed price (the "strike price") within a set period of time (the "duration"). The strike price may be smaller or greater than the current underlying security price (the "market price"). One option is a security, just like a stock or bond. Options are traded on a US stock exchange or bought/sold to a foreign broker. While an option grants one to leverage their cash (an option controls a higher stock value), it is high risk because it ends up expiring.

Understand the options trading risks. You can buy options speculatively or as a hedge against losses. Speculative purchases allow traders to make a great deal of money, but only if they can correctly predict the magnitude, timing, and direction of the price movement of the underlying security. This also opens up major profits and high trade fees for these traders. Especially for traders with novices, that makes trading options risky.

However, tools can also be used to protect your assets. For example, if you are worried that the price could drop unexpectedly, you may buy a put option to sell your shares of stock. This method of making use of options is very secure, as you can only lose the contract price.

Read and understand the booklet entitled "Standardised Options Characteristics and Risks".

This booklet has been written in accordance with SEC regulations. Brokerage companies distribute the booklet to those opening an option-trading account. In this book, you'll learn more about vocabulary options, the different types of options you can sell, exercise and settle options, options trader tax considerations, and the risks associated with options trading.

Comprehend the basic types of trades. There are two main types of trade options: calls and puts. Both show the right to either buy or trade a security at a given price within a defined period of time. The two types clearly consist of:

A "call" is the opportunity or right, but not the duty, to buy an asset at a given price within a specified time period. The buyer of a call hopes that the underlying stock price will rise during the option's term. For example, with a $100 hit, the buyer buys a call to a stock. The buyer expects the stock will rise (let's say, $105 per share), but he can purchase those stocks for $100. He can turn around if he wants, and sell those stocks for $105, thus making a profit. Otherwise, the purchaser will loosen the call bid costs.

A "put" is the option or a right, but not the commitment, to sell an asset at a specific price within a specified time period. The buyer of a put assumes that the price of the underlying stock will decline during the option's term.

In this case, the buyer will force the put option contract writer (seller) to purchase the asset at the present cost.

With the sale or purchase of a call or place, you can open a spot, close it by taking the opposite action, exercise it, or let it expire.

Learn to converse. Look up jargon for options-trading, arrange the words in a spreadsheet, print them out and begin researching.

Here are a few very essential terms:

One "resident" is someone who has purchased an option.

An "editor" is one who sold an option.

A "strike price" is the price the asset is purchased or sold at (depending on whether it's a call or a put). This is the price that a stock price has to go above (for calls) or below (for puts) before a profit option can turn.

The "expiry date" is the negotiated date by which the option owner will exercise his right to purchase or sell the security underlying it. The option expires after this date is reached, and the holder loses his / her right.

"In the money" is an expression used to indicate that the asset's market price is higher than the strike price (if it's a call) or lower than the strike price (if it's a put).

"Out of the pocket" is a term used to suggest that the asset's market price is lower than the strike price (if it's a call) or higher than the strike price (if it's a put).

Part 2 Preparing Options for Trade

A brokerage account is opened. If you need to trade options, you'll need to open a brokerage to enter your transactions — this may be online with sites such as www.iqoptionsbid.com or even a traditional broker account. You need to make sure to understand what's involved before you open a brokerage account.

Compare the commissions on trading options between different brokerages. Some companies don't even sell options trading commissions.

Do some online research and read the brokerage companies' reviews, which are on your shortlist. Learn from mistakes of other people, so you do not repeat them.

Look out for places and websites that trade scam. Often thoroughly research a platform before depositing any money. Avoid sites with negative reviews or fraudulent activity reported.

A cash account will only provide you to open a position by purchasing options. If you wish to sell an account opening option without having the underlying asset, you will need a margin account.

If you decide to trade online, make sure your online brokerage accepts safe payment forms such as a secure payment gateway for credit cards or a third-party payment system such as Skill, PayPal, Payoneer, bitcoin, etc.

Get trade options accepted. You will need to have your brokerage house approved before you can start buying and selling options. The brokerage companies that handle the account set limits based on account experience and money and each company has its own requirements to ensure that the customer knows what they are doing. Without an Options account, you can't write covered calls. Brokerage companies want to be sure that consumers understand the risks before they sell.

Covered call writing involves selling the right over the option term to buy the stock at a strike price. The buyer does have the right, not the seller. The stock must be in the account of the company and cannot be sold or exchanged while the call is outstanding.

Comprehend the technical analysis. Options are usually short-term investments, so in the near future you will be searching for price moves from the optioned security to gain a healthy return. In order to forecast those price fluctuations properly, you would need to grasp the basics of the technical analysis.

Get to know the levels of support and resistance. These are points where stock seldom falls below (support) or above (resistance).

Support is the level at which there has historically been a significant purchase of the security. Resistance is the price level where there have been significant sales of security in the past.

Understand volumetric value. When a stock moves in a particular direction with a lot of volume behind it, this usually means a strong trend, and can be an opportunity to make money.

Understand the trends of the Graph. History, even with stock prices, tends to repeat itself. There are unique trends you can look for in the movement of stock prices, which could mean where the price is going.

Learn about averages on the move. Often, when a stock price meets or falls below a specified moving average of previous prices. A moving average of 30 days is deemed more accurate than a moving average of 10 days.

Part 3 Comes with Trading Options

Start with "paper trading." Do not be tempted to gamble your hard-earned money on a technique you've just learned. Alternatively, opt for paper trading or work. Use a spreadsheet or practice the trading software to enter "pretend" trades. Then, for at least a few months, monitor your returns. If you make a decent return, you are ready to slowly work into real trading.

Paper trading is not the same as actual trading since psychological pressure or commissions are not involved. Understanding mechanics is a good way but not a predictor of real results.

Trading of real options is a very high risk that can result in significant losses to the seller. All you can afford to lose is trade with capital.

Use instructions with restrictions. Avoid paying options for market rates, as the execution price could be higher than expected. Instead, use limit orders to name your price and maximise your return.

Periodically reevaluate your plan. Determine if there is anything you can do to make your return better. Learn from mistakes but also repeat successful strategies. And keep your strategy focused; rather than diversifying, the traders focus on a few positions. No more than 10% of your investment portfolio should be available in options.

Part 4 Moving on to advanced Handling of Options

Join an online forum for traders with like-minded options. If you're dabbling with advanced trading options techniques, you'll find that valuable information source (and support, after some heartbreaking losses) is an online traders' forum just like you.

Find a forum so you can learn from other people's successes and, sadly, failures.

Consider other strategies when trading options. Once you've completed some successful trades, you can get approved for more complex trading options strategies. But start by trading them on paper as well. This will enable you to carry them out more easily in real trading.

One of the strategy is the "straddle," which requires trading on both sides of the market, purchasing a place and call option with both the same strike price and maturity date, so you can limit your exposure. This strategy is most successful when the market moves up and down, rather than in a single direction. It also runs the risk of being exerciser on only one side.

A close strategy is the "strip," which is like the mount, but is a "bearish" strategy on a downward price movement with double the earning power. In its execution, it is similar to the straddle but with twice as many options purchased on the downside (place options).

Read on to the Greeks. Once you've mastered basic trading options and decided to move on to more complicated trading options, you'll need to know about the so-called "Greeks. These are measures that traders use to optimise their returns.

An option with a .5 delta would have half that of the underlying asset in motion. If the stock moves $1.00, the price of the option moves $0.50.

The gamma-the rate that the delta will change, based on a stock price change of $1.

Theta - the option price's so-called 'time decay.' It measures how much the price worsens as the option approaches expiration.

Vega-the amount that will change the option price based on the volatility of the underlying asset.

2.2. WHAT KIND OF ACCOUNT SHOULD BE OPENED TO BEGIN OPTION TRADING?

Possibly no customer is more valuable to an online broker than an options trader for active traders. Options trades deliver much higher profit margins to brokers than stock trades, and thus rivalry is intense in attracting these customers. This kind of market atmosphere is great for investors since product innovation, and competitive pricing comes with healthy competition.

Best Websites for Trading Options.

Hereby are the best trading platform options, which are based on over 100 variables.

- E*TRADE-Best for Overall Options
- Trade-Station-Low cost, platform major
- TD Ameritrade-Tools with Best Choices
- Interactive Brokers-Perfect for Experts
- Charles Schwab-Forms of One Order

E*THREAD

Constructed as a web-based platform, Power E*TRADE innovates and delivers speed, user-friendliness, and the tools needed for successful traders. Power E*TRADE once again won our award, "Best Web-based Platform," in our 2020 Review. E*TRADE also gets hold of our top spot for trading options.

Commerce-station

Trade-Station shines as a pioneer in the trading technology. Trading options is a breeze using Option-Station Pro, a built-in tool designed for streamlined trading and robust analysis within the Trade-Station desktop platform.

Custom grouping for current positions, streaming real-time Greeks, and advanced position analysis, to name a few, include the options tool capabilities.

Brokers Interactive

Trading tools are designed for professional options traders within the Trader Workstation (TWS) platform. Interactive brokers are designed for traders, ranging from also trading to Options Strategy Lab, Volatility Lab, Risk Navigator, Market Scanner, Strategy Builder, and Portfolio Builder. Options commissions begin at $.65 per contract, with a minimum of $1.00 and no maximum.

What's the Best Trading Options Platform?

The best options trading platform provides low prices, feature-rich trading tools, and rigorous analysis. Power E*TRADE is our all-around top pick for options trading in 2020. The web-based Power E*TRADE platform provides all the resources that a trader would like and shows them in a beautiful way. My two favourites are Snapshot Analysis and Strategy Seek.

Types of Trading Accounts

Trading accounts, and account types, can vary greatly from one broker to another. The best choice isn't always obvious, from cash and margin accounts to retail or technical accounts.

Here we will discuss all the account choices and clarify your preferences, including some of the broker-specific "VIP" or "Cash" accounts.

Retail Business Accounts

Retail dealers are individual traders with no direct working day trading experience and often rely on the information and education obtained from broker sites. Most retail traders may execute their own cash trades and may trade in a variety of securities, such as stocks, forex or options.

When considering the numerous trading accounts available to retail traders, it is important to shop around for the most suitable online broker. Various brokers charge various network charges, and these can include a network or commission fee per transaction.

Trade costs are often blended into the 'flat' buy and sell and are not seen as fees.

In addition, many sites include daily purchasing tips and a valuable knowledge base that can expand retail traders' education.

ESMA Limits

In an attempt to reduce losses, the European Securities and Markets Authority (ESMA) have placed a number of restrictions on retail traders. Which one includes the maximum leverage for?

- 30:1 (Forex accounts) on all major currency pairs
- 20:1 on major or gold indices
- 10:1 on all products, except gold
- 5:1 On Stocks
- On crypto currencies 2:1

These limits will apply only to EEA trading accounts, using a European regulated broker. Popular trading regions listed as 'Unregulated' by ESMA include Singapore, Australia, India, and Canada-they are still well-regulated regions, but not under the control of the ESMA.

Bronze, Silver, Gold

Retail traders may find that different broker brands offer regular traders different incentives, and these usually apply to the account level. Traders' attaining Bronze, Gold, or VIP status accounts from their broker, for example, would have different terms and conditions for other traders.

This could include lower rates for transactions, higher-speed access to a premium server, or even a dedicated account manager. All these incentives can be a valuable account reward for day traders, but they are still not equal to a skilled trading account being offered.

You have the possibility to set up a cash account or a margin account.

Explained Cash accounts

Cash accounts are capped, so only the funds deposited to the account can be used by traders. This can be very useful to beginner traders because they will prevent any loss of inexpensive money.

Margin Exchange

If you open a trading margin account, the broker will give you a line of credit. This may help to maximise any future profits, but it also means traders are at risk of losses, which may not be affordable. These types of accounts are generally more strictly regulated, as most brokers require a minimum investment before any margin trading. It is also very likely that the broker could make a margin call in which a higher deposit is needed to cover any potential cash losses.

Trained Corporate Accounting

Registered trading accounts are open only to traders with proven skill levels that also have a certain amount of available investment capital, usually at least £500,000. With these accounts, limitations are withdrawn from the European Securities and Markets Authority (ESMA), and traders can exploit up to 1:5,000 of funding for a variety of trades. However, it is important to record that for skilled traders, there is no form of regulatory security in place.

It is believed that these seasoned investors with regulatory constraints are able to control their own affairs and choices. This involves the right to exchange items of greater risk, such as binary options.

No Outside Europe constraints

In order to avoid any ambiguity, it should be noted that ESMA constraints apply only within the EU, while leverage rates are unaffected in non-European and non-regulated jurisdictions.

What is the reason for this? This way, several European brokers have made the decision to move offshore after the ESMA implemented stringent leverage regulations. Traders selling binary options have long traded offshore, and several forex traders and CFD brokers are now following suit.

Brokers offering up to 1:1,000 leverage tend to be located in the Australian Area (ASIC Regulated), Seychelles, and Belize. In the first case, retail traders would find it appropriate to begin trading at leverage rates of about 1:10 or 1:25 to reduce potential losses.

Ways to escape ESMA restrictions

As already noted, one way to escape the leverage conditions set by ESMA is to turn to brokers based on locations that are not impacted by EU legislation. However, it should be understood that in order to protect retail traders and rising financial risks, these regulations were positioned in place. Definitely, traders should not feel tempted to move to unregulated brokers to circumvent leverage laws, since this is risky, and there are other choices.

One option is to find out if your current broker already has brands of an offshore or non-EU subsidiary. Many brokers have lots of controlled brands under their "summit," so it's quite possible to move your retail account into a jurisdiction outside the EU or offshore. You would just need to contact your current broker to find out more about any other brands that they are selling within appropriate locations.

Another option is to look at the introduction of new products and alternative goods into the market. For example, at the time the binary options trade was banned in the EU, IQ Options launched FX Options, and this is very similar in character.

Finally, retail traders may look to become skilled traders looking for a way to escape the ESMA bans. Not all retail traders will have that potential, but the downside of becoming a skilled trader is that there are no regulatory safeguards.

Professional traders will need at least two years of trading experience in a relevant financial position and a minimum level of funding available, usually around £500,000, but this can be divided between multiple accounts. Attaining the rank of a skilled trader ensures that greater leveraging opportunities can open up on binary stocks, forex, and CFDs.

Many forms of Account

Some of the other business account types on the UK market include PAMM accounts and Micro Trading accounts.

Contacts PAMM

PAMM accounts are relatively new for forex trading and are a perfect solution for investors with time constraints. These accounts use a mutual cash pool for forex trading. Trades are made by seasoned traders, and usually, investors should be able to choose the trader they want to treat.

PAMM stands for "Control of the percentage distribution modules." This model spreads the sizes of trades according to the percentage of allocations.

A MAM account does something similar but enables management of several trading accounts by the fund manager.

Micro-Commerce Accounts

Micro-dealing refers to the lower CFD and currency exchange trading. They are a good way to start forex trading and for seasoned traders who don't have a lot of time to commit to transactions. Smaller lot sizes and margin specifications make them appealing to a given market for beginners or those that are new to trade.

Accounts under Charge

Managed accounts, especially accounts controlled from forex, can be a risky field. To hand over responsibility for trading to someone else there is plenty of risk. If the broker also employs the individual, then there is a conflict of interest as well. Look out for false claims, or instant wealth assurances.

PAMM and MAM accounts are less risky because they are more tightly regulated, and because traders make money based on volume rather than losing trades, the conflict of interest is eliminated.

Some high-level accounts, such as VIP accounts, may require an account manager-but this is not the same as an account managed.

Social trading and copy trading are not really accounts that are managed, although they can promote automated trading.

Taking responsibility for your own trading is usually the safest option.

Accounts of ECN

An ECN account allows you direct access to the markets as a trader, without going through a market maker (as most brokers do). This usually means the tightest spreads but also dynamic networks for trading. IC Markets is an example of a broker on ECN.

DMA-Easy exposure to the sector

A DMA account is somewhat similar to an ECN account, as the name implies, but ECN trades are put directly on the market through an anonymous network, whereas DMA accounts have contracts with a particular liquidity provider.

2.3. CORE ELEMENTS IN OPTIONS TRADING
Elements a Successive Tradition Plan

Perhaps the single most important aspect of profitably engaging the financial markets is developing a comprehensive trading plan. A regulatory approach to active trade fosters is a clear dialog between the trader and the marketplace.

Entering the active trading arena without having a strategy first is like driving a car fitted with a broken windshield — you can get from point A to point B, but the chances of doing so safely are drastically reduced. By investing the resources needed to build and implement a viable trading plan, a trader will be able to avoid the many stumbling blocks that stand on the way of marketplace success.

What is Included in a Successful Trading Plan?

It's a method to transact successfully. No matter how complex a strategy is or how vast the available resources are, in the sense of any trading plan, a trader must clearly identify three distinct elements:

- Entering and leaving the business

- Risk

- Psychology

Getting each of these concepts fleshed out in-depth is important for the development of a systematic market approach. Every subject is interconnected to the others. If one item is missing, it jeopardises the integrity of the entire trade program.

1. Entry and Departure to the market

The art of understanding when and how to trade is at its heart active trade. Implementation of a set of specific guidelines governing market entry and exit is essential for competent trading.

Executing a trade is a fairly simple act. A simple mouse-click on a DOM order or a broker call could open or close a market place. However, a key driver of success is the methodology behind the decision to buy or sell a security.

A viable strategy clearly defining business entry and exit gives the Trading Plan the following attributes:

Promotes continuity and productivity relating to trade

Sets up a statistically verifiable record

Reduces the effect of greed and fear on profitability

A crucial part of any successful trading plan is a thorough understanding of market entry and exit. In order to maintain a viable "head" over the competition, consistent and successful marketplace habits are necessary.

2. Managing threats

Aggressive risk management is an integral part of efficiency relating to trade.

Every time traders enter the market, in the hopes of achieving a return, they put capital into harm's way. While danger is unavoidable, it is not reckless trade.

Professionals in the industry often mention risk management as the prime factor in a successful trade. Here are several factors that traders need to consider when discussing the role of risk in any trading plan:

It is important to respect the inherent volatility of the product being targeted.

Prudent money management ensures that liquidity for the account is maintained.

Risk and reward balance favour the efficient use of usable capital resources.

Risk is an entity that is ever-evolving and can change without notice. The trader, however, is in full control of how much risk a particular trade presumes. A robust trading plan ensures that capital is used effectively in the face of any unforeseen adversity.

3. The Psychology of Good Trading

A key element in performance optimisation is the adoption of the trading methodology that is most suitable for one's psychological makeup.

Specific sets of skills and predispositions better lend themselves to certain techniques than others. To put it simply, not every trading type is a good fit for every individual.

Typically, in a successful trading plan these attributes are present:

User-friendly: The purpose of the trading plan must be clear and meaningful to the user, execution being of second nature.

Comprehensible: The trader must be comfortable with the technology and methods which govern the implementation of a strategy.

Promotes discipline: The plan must be trusted by the trader in order for a plan to deliver up to its capabilities. This ensures there is consistent execution of the strategy over time.

The realisation of steady market gains is a product of tenacity, dedication, and competence. If the user has a reason for the trading plan, seamless execution is possible. Any conflicts surrounding plan implementation are eliminated when fully addressing the psychological needs of the trader.

Building a viable market entry and exit strategy, risk accounting, and overcoming psychological barriers are integral parts of a robust trading plan. If you neglect one of these items, performance is sure to suffer.

If you are interested in exploring what a fully customised strategy can do for your portfolio, check out the options available for online futures trading at Daniels Trading. A veteran in the futures industry for more than 20 years, Daniels Trading has a vast collection of resources at the ready to help you achieve your market-related goals.

2.4. BEST OPTIONS TRADING PLATFORMS

Trading options is a somewhat high-risk investment world area where you can pay on a future date for the option of buying or selling a particular security at a set price. Based on market price fluctuations for those securities, the value of the options will rise and fall until their maturity date.

If you'd like to trade options, you'll need a brokerage account that supports options. - The platform is rare and has its own pros and cons, so before you get started, it's best to understand what you want in an account and platform choices. Follow in to learn more about the best trading platforms options and which might best suit your trading needs choices.

Best Package: TD Ameritrade

Thanks to a combination of fair pricing, excellent beginner tools, and a top-of-the-line trading platform that works well for experts and experienced traders, TD Ameritrade takes the top spot within this ranking. Wherever you are on your trading options travel, TD Ameritrade has something for everyone.

TD Ameritrade trades cost $6.95 per trading plus $0.75 cents per contract. There is no minimum account. The site offers an on-going deal where you get 60 days of commission-free shares, ETF, and options trading with a $3,000 or more deposit. You get extra bonuses with larger deposits that open.

Beginners have a wide range of resources, which are great for options and other strategies for investing and trading. The Think or Swim platform gives you quality Wall Street at a Main Street price for experienced traders.

Nice for None: Robin Hood

You can't make it any cheaper than free. While some professional traders aren't happy with how trades are handled and processed at Robin Hood, getting started with less risk is an excellent platform, especially for beginners. With no trading fee, options can be purchased and sold without risking anything more than the initial investment.

Robin Hood is a web-first platform, and when it comes to educational and research tools, it doesn't offer much. But if you are reading a book on options and want to try your hand as a hobbyist, Robin Hood can handle your needs for sure.

Robin hood also provides commission-free stock trades, ETFs, a limited number of crypto currencies, and a limited number of ADRs (American Depository Receipts — a kind of stock listing for a foreign company in the United States). Because it is firstly mobile, it offers great real-time notifications on the platform for both investments and trades.

Expert's Best: Trade Station

Trade Station started as a software company for traders, and although it has grown over time, it has remained true to its initial principles of trading. Trade Station is a great choice if you want qualified data and high-speed commercial execution on an expert-level platform.

Trade Station charges $5 for each trade plus $0.50 for every contract. However, it also offers unbundled, per-contract piecing. Professional and high-volume traders can do better with the flat rate cost of $1 per contract instead of the base + most brokerages charge per contract fee.

Although it doesn't offer as much for beginner traders and new traders, you could have no problems hosting a family office or business portfolio on Trade Station. In reality, its tools are so strong that it sells a lot of them to professional investors with accounts at other brokers for a fee. You'll get those tools for free with an active Trade Station account.

Only be aware of the minimum balance of $2,000 or five trades per year to escape an annual account fee of $95.

Charles Schwab: Best for New Traders

Charles Schwab delivers a great product of excellent customer service all around. Trades are $.95 each and $0.65 cents per agreement once you open a new account. For two years, first-time clients get 500 commission-free trades when you deposit $100,000 or more into a new account.

Schwab gives the chance to use above-average offerings in research and education. It also gives you a very good desktop, web, and mobile trading platform. It is one of the finest overall brokerages for a wide range of investment and trading needs, even outside of the options.

With the extensive educational and research content library, you can enter the world of high-speed trading options with your eyes wide open to all risks and opportunities. With the being said, for even the most experienced traders, the competitive costs and the quality trading platforms make it a worthwhile consideration. Accounts require a minimum of $1,000 to trade access options.

Best for Low and No Minimum Cost: Ally Invest

Ally Invest is yet another low-cost brokerage, which is best known for its Ally Bank counterpart. As with the bank, Ally Invest offers a lineup of easy-to-understand and low-fee brokerage. Trades are $4.95 per contract plus $0.65 cents each. There is no minimum account. You can obtain up to $3,500 bonus cash with a current promotion, depending on the size of your deposit. With the low investment, you can start learning more about Ally without thinking about major minimum balances or fees. But even some more seasoned traders would be pleased with the low costs and a wide variety of options traders focused services.

Highlights include a powerful trading platform and useful charts, data, and analytics to help build your trading strategy for options. In the discount brokerage environment, you are not always able to take a broker's value from its trading fees. That is certainly the case at Alliance.

Best Rate per Trade: Digital Brokers

In case you're an active trader who likes to do regular, small businesses, Interactive Brokers may be the best choice. There is no pre-trade charge and fees on options amount to $0.70 cents per offer. High volume traders with 100,000 + contracts per month will apply for a lower price down to $0.15 cents per contract.

This brokerage also provides competitive rates for the active stock and ETF traders. Non-US options are subject to differing pricing.

This brokerage is not ideal for conservative investors with few trades per annum or a broad balance. To avoid an activity fee, the account requires a heavy $100,000 minimum balance or $10 in commissions per month. The activity fee is the difference between your trading commissions and $10 per month, totalling a minimum monthly charge of $10. The account charges a rate of $20 more if you do not keep at least $2,000 in the account's equities.

If you have the appetite for at least $10 a month in trades and/or are willing to meet a total of $100,000, Digital Brokers has excellent trading platforms. These tools include a natural language bot that will position orders based on your instructions and a mobile platform of professional quality.

Best value for money: Light speed

Light speed is a brokerage with a focus on experienced and active traders. Light speed pays $0 per trade, and $0.60 per export, with a total of $1 per trade. Tiered pricing begins at +500 contracts a month. The discounted rates vary from $0.20 cents at 100,000 + contracts per month to $0.50 cents at 500-2,000 contracts per month; it depends on your volume.

Light speed offers platforms for professional-level trading. The Livevol X options platform provides automated order execution, analysis, custom templates, historical data analytics, and other useful features. Like competing platforms, most common account needs can be handled right in the desktop, web, or mobile platforms.

This brokerage isn't as open-minded as others on our list, so if you're brand-new to options trading, you should look elsewhere. But if you are experienced and want professional equipment, then at Light speed, you will find anything you need to whet your appetite. With low pricing for traders with high-volume options, you can find the right home for your brokering options.

Best for Your Skills Growing: E-Trade

E-Trade is the oldest online brokerage and has a long history of supporting traders at both beginner and expert level. You have the possibility to discover a wide range of data and research tools through his dedicated Options House platform. These include tools to construct sophisticated chains of options and ladders to trading.

Although it's a discount brokerage, commissions aren't the lowest on the list. Trades cost 6.95 dollars, plus 0.75 cents per deal. Some discounts are, however, applicable for high volume traders. Equity and index options are down to $4.95 per trade and $0.50 per contract with 30 trades or more per quarter.

With a new account bringing in a $10,000 or more balance, you'll get up to $600 in free trade and 60 days of commission-free trade. That's quite a good deal for you to get started. Consider always with E-Trade and others how, over time, trade fees cut into your profits.

CHAPTER 3: OPTION TRADING STRATEGIES

Option strategies are the concurrent and purchase, or sale of one or more options that differ in one or more variables of the options. Call options, simply known as calls, offer purchasers the right to purchase a specific stock at the strike price of that option. Conversely, putting options simply called puts gives the buyer the right to sell a particular stock at the strike price of the option. This is often done to gain access to a specific type of opportunity or risk as part of a trading strategy while removing other risks. A very simple strategy could simply be buying or selling one choice; however, option strategies often refer to a combination of buying and/or selling options at the same time.

Options strategies allow traders to benefit from market sentiment (i.e., bullish, bearish, or neutral) driven changes in the underlying assets. In the specific case of neutral approaches, they can be further graded as bullish on volatility, calculated by the Greek lowercase letter sigma (ÿ), and bearish on volatility. Traders can also benefit from time decrease, determined by the Greek letter theta (Theta of uppercase) when the stock market is low in volatility. The option positions used in calls and puts can be long and/or short.

Bubble strategies

Bullish options strategies are used when options traders foresee upward movement of the underlying stock price. They may also use Theta (time decay) with a bullish/bearish combo called a Calendar Spread when it is expected to move sideways. The trader may also predict how high the stock price can go and the time frame in which the rally can take place to select the optimum trading strategy to purchase a bullish option.

The bullishness of selling options strategies, used by most options traders, is simply buying a call option.

The business is always on the move. During that period of time, it is completely up to the trader to work out what approach suits the markets. Traders with moderately bullish options typically set a target price for the bull run and use bull spreads to minimise costs or remove risk altogether. There are restricted opportunities for risk trading, using the correct strategy. Although for some of these techniques, maximum profit is capped, they usually cost less to employ for a given nominal exposure number. There are several solutions that have unlimited potential with limited risk to the up or downside if done correctly. The spread of the bull call and the spread of the bull put are common examples of fairly bullish strategies.

Mildly bullish trading strategies are options that compose money as long as the underlying asset price does not fall to the strike price by the expiration date of the option. Such tactics may also provide defence against the downside. Writing calls covered off-the-money is a perfect example of such a technique. The purchaser of the protected call charges a premium for the right to buy the assets you already own, at the strike price (rather than the market price). This is the process of how traders hedge a stock they own when it's been going against them for a while.

Bring on tactics

Bearish options strategies are employed when options traders expect the downward movement of the underlying stock price. It chooses the best trading strategy, it is important to determine how low the stock price will go, and the time period in which the decline will eventually occur. Selling a Bearish option is also another form of strategy that "credits" the trader. That needs an account with a margin.

The most bearish of trading options strategies is the simple strategy of buying or selling that the majority of traders use.

The market will make steep moves downwards. Traders with moderate bearish options usually set a target price for the expected decline, and use bear spreads with the goal of reducing costs. This strategy has limited profit potential, but when done correctly, it significantly reduces risk.

The spread of the bear call and the bear put spread common examples of bearish techniques of moderation.

The mildly bearish trading strategy is an options strategy that composes money, given that the underlying asset does not rise to the strike price by the expiry date of the options. You can, however, add more options to the current position and move to a more forward position based on "Theta" Time Decay. These strategies can also provide slight protection for the upside. Bearish strategies generally yield benefit, with less risk of loss.

Strategies Neutral or Non-directional

Neutral options trading strategies are used when the options trader does not know if the price of the underlying asset will go up or down. They are also known as non-directional strategies since the opportunity for profit doesn't depend on whether the underlying price will rise or fall. Rather, the right neutral strategy to employ depends on the predicted volatility of the stock price at the root.

Examples of Tactics Neutral are:

Guts-buy (long intestine) or sell (short intestine) a pair of ITMs (in cash) put and call (compared to a strangle where OTM places and calls are trading);

Butterfly-a technique of balanced options mixing spreads of bulls and bears.

Long butterfly increase uses four options contracts with equal expiration but three distinct strike prices to create a variety of prices from which the strategy will profit.

Straddle-an option strategy under which the buyer keeps both a call position and positions the same price and expiry date, charging all premiums (a long straddle).

Strangle-where you buy a put below the stock and a call above the stock, with a benefit if the stock goes below either strike price (long strangle).

Danger reversal-simulates the movement of an underlying in a way that these are often referred to as synthetic long or synthetic short positions depending on the position you are in;

Collar-buy the underlying option and then buy it concurrently below the current price (floor) and offer a call option above the current price (cap);

Fence-buy the underlying options on either side of the price at the same time to limit the number of potential returns;

Iron butterfly-offer two overlapping vertical credit spreads but one of the vertical spreads is on the call side and the other on the put side;

Iron condor-buying a put spread at the same time and spreading a call with the same expiration and four different hits.

An iron condor can be the hope of as selling a strangle rather of buying, and therefore restricting the risk on both the call side and putting side by building a vertical spreading bull and a vertical spreading bear call;

Jade Lizard-a vertical bull spread created using call options, with the addition of a put option offered at a strike price lower than the call spread strike prices in the same expiry cycle;

Calendar spread-the one-month purchase of an option and the reciprocal selling of an option for a debit at the same (and underlying) strike price in a previous month.

Option Trading Strategies

Options are conditional derivative contracts that allows contract buyers (option holders) to purchase or sell a security at a price chosen. Option buyers are paid the sellers for such a right by an amount called a "premium." If market prices for option holders are unfavourable, they will cause the option to expire worthlessly, thereby ensuring that the losses are not higher than the premium. By comparison, sellers of options (contract writers) expect greater risk than buyers of the option, which is why they claim this as premium. Options are split into the options "call" and "put." With a call option, the contract buyer acquires the right to purchase the underlying asset at a predetermined price in the future, which is called the exercise price or the strike price.

The buyer acquires the right, with a put option, to sell the underlying asset at the agreed price in the future.

Why Trade Options Instead of Direct Assets?

Trading options come with some benefits. The Chicago Board of Options Exchange (CBOE) is the world's largest exchange with options on a wide range of single stocks, ETFs, and indexes. Traders can build option strategies ranging from buying or selling one option to very complex ones involving multiple simultaneous option positions.

3.1 OPTIONS TRADING STRATEGIES

Often traders jump into options with little understanding of options strategies. There are a lot of strategies that limit risk and maximise return. Traders will learn with a little effort on how to maximise the versatility and power options offered. Keeping that in mind, we've put this primer together, which should shorten the learning curve and point you in the right direction.

1. Covered Call

One strategy with calls is to simply buy a naked call option. Another option would be to create a simple, protected call or buy-write structure. This is a very popular strategy, as it generates revenue and reduces some risk of being the stock alone for long. The trade-off is that you must be eager to sell your shares at a fixed price the price for the short strike. To execute the strategy, you buy the underlying stock as you would normally do, and at the same time write (or sell) a call option on the same shares.

In this example, on stock, we are using a call option, which represents 100 stock shares per call option. You sell one call option against it at the same time for every 100 shares of stock that you buy. It is called a covered call because if stock rockets higher in price, the long stock position covers your short call. This strategy could be used by investors when they have a short-term stock position and a neutral opinion on its direction. They may look to generate revenue (through the sale of the call premium) or protect against a potential decline in the value of the underlying stock.

Note in the P&L graph above how the negative P&L from the call is offset by the position of the long share as the stock price increases. Because you receive a premium from the sale of the call, as the stock moves upwards through the strike price, the premium you received allows you to sell your stock effectively at a higher level than the strike price (strike + premium received). P&L graph of the covered call is very similar to the P&L graph of a short naked put.

2. Married Put

In a married put strategy, an investor buys an asset (in this example, stock shares), and at the same time, purchases put options for an equivalent number of shares. The holder of a put option is entitled to sell stock at the price of the strike. Each contract valued 100 shares. When holding stock, the reason and investor would use this strategy is simply to protect their downside risk. This strategy works just like an insurance policy and establishes a price floor that should pay the price of the stock drop sharply.

An object of a married put would be in the case that an investor was buying 100 stock shares and buying one put option at the same time. This strategy is appealing because if a negative event occurs, an investor is protected to the downside. At the same time, if the stock increases in value, the investor would be sharing in all of the upsides. If the stock does not fall, the only downside to this strategy will occur; in this case the investor will lose the premium paid for the put option.

The dashed line in the P&L graph above is the long-stock position. Combined with the long put and long stock positions, you can see that the losses are limited as the stock price falls. Yet the stock is involved upside-down above the premium spent on the put. P&L graph of the married put looks similar to the P&L graph of a long call.

3. Spreading Bull Call

In a strategy for spreading a bull call, an investor would purchase calls at a common strike price at the same time and sell the same number of calls at a higher strike price. Both of these call options will have the same expiry and underlying asset. This form of vertical spread strategy is normally used when an investor is optimistic about the underlying and expects the asset's price to rise moderately. The investor limits his / her upside on an exchange but reduces the net premium paid outright compared to purchasing a naked call option.

You can observe in the P&L graph above that this is a bullish strategy, so the trader wants the stock to rise in price to make a profit on the trade. When putting on a bull call spread, the trade-off is that your upside is limited, while your premium spending is reduced. If outright calls are costly, the sale of higher strike calls against them is one way to offset the higher premium. This is how a spread of the bull call is built up.

4. Place Bear Put

Another form of vertical spread is a bear put spread strategy. In this strategy, the investor will purchase set options at a specific strike price at the same time and sell the same number of puts at a lower strike price. Both options are for the same underlying asset and have the same date of expiry.

This strategy is applied when the trader is bearish and expects a fall in the price of the underlying asset. It offers limited losses, but at the same time it can also limit gains.

You can observe in the P&L graph above that this is a bearish strategy, so you need the stock to go down to profit. When using a bear put spread the trade-off is that your upside is minimal, but your premium spent is that. If outright puts are costly, one way to offset the high premium is by selling against them the lower strike puts. This is the method of how a spread of the bear put is built.

5. Protective Edge

A safe collar strategy is implemented by buying an out-of-the-money put option and writing an out-of-the-money call option for the same underlying asset and expiration simultaneously. This strategy is often employed by investors after substantial gains have been made from a long position in a stock. This mix of options allows investors to have security against the downside (long puts to lock in profits), while having the trade-off of being theoretically forced to sell shares at a higher price (selling higher = more benefit than at modern stock level). A simple case would be if an investor is at $50 for 100 long IBM shares, and as of January 1st, IBM has risen to $100. The investor could create a defensive collar by selling one IBM call on March 15th 105 and purchasing one IBM call on March 95 at the same time.

The trader is covered below $95 until March 15, possibly having an obligation to sell his / her stock at $105 with the trading bid.

You can observe in the P&L graph above, that the protective collar is a mixture of a covered call and a long put. This is a fair-trading setup, ensuring you are safe in case stock declines, but with the trade-off of having the legal obligation to sell your long stock during the short call hit. The lender should be happy to do it again, though, as they have already experienced gains in the underlying shares.

6. Short walk

A long straddle options strategy is when a lender buys a call at the same time and puts an option on the same underlying asset, with the same price and expiration date. An investor will frequently use this strategy when he or she believes that the price of the underlying asset will move significantly out of a range, but is not sure of which direction the move takes. This strategy allows the investor the ability to make theoretically unlimited gains, while the maximum loss is limited only to the combined cost of both options contracts.

Note how there are two break-even points in the P&L graph above. This strategy is considered to be successful when the stock makes a big push one way or the other. For the investor doesn't matter which way the stock moves, only because it is a bigger move than the investor's total premium paid for the structure.

7. Strangle Long

The investor selects an out-of-the-money call option in a long strangle options strategy, and an out-of-the-money option places simultaneously on the same underlying asset and expiry date. An investor using this strategy believes the price of the underlying asset will be experiencing a very big movement but is unsure of which direction the move will take. For example, this could be a wager for a company's earnings release or an FDA event for a health care stock. Losses for all options are limited to the costs (or the premium spent). Strangles will almost always be cheaper than straddles because the purchased options are out of money.

Note how there are two break-even points in the P&L graph above. When the stock makes a really big push in one direction or the other, this technique is profitable. Again, for the investor doesn't matter which way the stock goes, just that it's a bigger step than the investor's overall premium charged for the structure.

8. Butterfly Spread Long Call

All the strategies required a combination of two different positions or contracts up to this point. A trader can mix both a bull spread strategy, and a bear spread strategy in a long butterfly spread using call options and will use three different strike prices. All options are for the same underlying date of asset and expiry.

For example, buying an in-the-money call option at a lower strike price, while selling two at-the-money call options, and buying one out-of-the-money call option, may create a long butterfly spread. A healthy distribution of butterflies will have the same wing widths. This example is called a "call fly," which leads to a net debit. An investor would enter a long butterfly call spread when they think the stock isn't going to move much by expiry.

Note how the maximum gain is made in the P&L graph above when the stock remains unchanged until expiry (right at the ATM strike). The further away from ATM strikes the stock shifts, the greater the negative P&L shift. Maximum loss happens when the stock settles at or below the lower strike, or when the stock settles at or above the higher strike call. This strategy has both the upside limited and the downside limited.

Notice how the maximum gain is built when the stock remains at the call's at-the-money strikes and puts outsold in the P&L graph above. A maximum gain is earned a total net premium. Maximum loss occurs when the stock measures above the long call strike or below the long-put price.

9. Condor made of iron

The iron condor is considered to be an even more fascinating tactic. In this strategy, a bull put spread, and a bear call spread is held simultaneously by the investor.

The iron condor is built by selling one out-of-the-money put and buying one out-of-the-money put of a lower strike (bull put spread), and by selling one out-of-the-money call and buying one out-of-the-money call of a higher strike (bear call spread). Both options have the same cease date and are available on the same underlying asset. Usually, the sides of the put and call have the same width of spread. This trading strategy receives a net premium on the structure and is designed to leverage a low volatility stock. Many traders like this type of trade because of its perceived high probability of a small amount of premium being earned.

Note how the maximum gain is made when the stock remains within a relatively broad trading range in the P&L graph above, which would result in the investor earning the total net credit received when building the trade. The further the stock moves through the short strikes (lower for the put, higher for the call), the greater the loss until the maximum loss is achieved. Typically, the average loss is slightly higher than the maximum benefit, which makes sense intuitively, considering that there is a greater chance of the system ending with a small profit.

10. Butterfly made of iron

The iron butterfly is the final options strategy we will be demonstrating. An investor will trade an at-the-money put and buy an out-of-the-money put in this strategy, while also selling an at-the-money call and buying an out-of-the-money call. Both options have the same cease date and are available on the same underlying asset. Although similar to a spread of a butterfly, the difference in this strategy is that it uses both calls and places, as opposed to one or the other.

This strategy combines the sale of an at-the-money straddle and the purchase of protective "wings essentially." You can also think of the figure as two spreads. It is normal for both spreads to be of the same width. The lengthy out-of-the-money call defends against the endless downside. The long-out-of-the-money put defends against downside from the short-positioned attack to zero. Profit and loss are both narrow within a specific range, depending on the options used for the strike prices—investors like this income strategy, and the greater likelihood of a small gain with a non-volatile stock.

Note how the maximum gain is made when the stock remains at the call's at-the-money strikes and puts outsold in the P&L graph above. Maximum gain is received total net premium. When the stock moves over the long call strike or below the long-put strike, maximum loss occurs.

81

5 Easy to Learn Options Trading Strategies

Strategies on Best Options:

- Fundamental strategies, including long calls and long puts
- Strategies for defence include collar strategies and defensive puts
- Strategies for improvement including cash-covered puts and covered calls
- Vertical strategies, including long call and short call spreads
- Calendar techniques like long/short timelines

What are the Options?

To summarise everything, options are contracts among two parties where one party gives the other party the right to buy or sell an asset at a given price (known as the strike price) up to the date of expiry specified.

The amount paid is known as the prime for this right.

For more information on how to start trading options, check out Benzinga.

Contract Incentive Forms

Even though most people think of stocks when considering options, there is a wide range of instruments that include contract options:

- Materials
- Undertakings
- ETF
- Indices
- Rohstoffs
- Curricula
- Zukunft

Many derivatives include

1. Grundlagen Approaches

Most people start with strategies on some easier choices. You can learn Benzinga's guide on the difference between calls for more and puts.

Long-distance call

A simple strategy where an investor bets the stock, by expiration, will surpass the strike price.

Position: Buy a call option or more

Bias: Evil

Risk: Pay the premium

Potential for profit: Exclusive

Prices for break-even: strike price + premium charged

Registered accounts: Simple margin, including self-managed investment accounts

Key insights: When there is a lower implied volatility index (IV Index), the call options will be less expensive.

Place long

A basic strategy, in which an investor bets the stock, by expiration, will go below the strike price.

Position: Buy one or more Put Options

Bias: Boredom

Risk: Pay the premium

Potential for profit: Exclusive

Break-even price: the price of strike-premium charged

Registered accounts: Simple margin, including self-managed investment accounts

Main insights: Placing options would almost always cost more than the equivalent call options.

2. Protection Strategy

Protection strategies are used by investors to hedge or protect current positions within their portfolio.

Necklace

A technique that caps the upside but also downside potential used when you already own stock.

Position: Selling one call option and purchasing one put option

Odds: Neutral

Risk: Difference between the current price and the price of the put strike

Potential for profit: Difference between the current price and the demand for call strike

Price break-even: somewhere between calling and selling strikes

Registered accounts: Simple margin, including self-managed investment accounts

Key insights: The collar fits well with highly paid dividend inventories. Since the position is neutral, both upsides and the downside are capped, while being secured, investors will continue to receive dividends.

Putting defence on

- Usage of a put to guard along with the current role.

Position: Buy one put option while the stock is long

Bias: Boredom

Risk: Pay the premium

Potential for profit: an appreciation of stock capital-premium charged

Prices for breaks: current stock price + premium payable

Registered accounts: Simple margin, including self-managed investment accounts

Key insights: it would be good do so when purchasing defensive puts before the markets start to turn down dramatically, and when the IV index is lower.

3. Building Strategies

If you already own stock or have a stock that you wish to own, improvement strategies would allow you to make money from stocks that you already own or add to your portfolio:

Put on cash covered

- Sale of a put where cash is reserved to cover the total amount of stock that could potentially be purchased at the price of the strike.

Position: Sale of one or more placed contracts for each contract, with sufficient cash equal to 100 shares multiplied by the strike price.

Bias: Evil

Risk: stock price below the put strike price anywhere-premium paid

Profit potential: Premium paid

Break-even price: the price of strike-premium charged

Eligible accounts: Basic margin, including self-directed investment accounts with further approvals

Key insights: Most leaders use cash-covered puts as a way to gather some extra premium on a stock they already want to buy.

You can also use this strategy as a bullish bet when a stock is already in-the-money.

Covered Call

- Sale of a call option against a stock value that you're in your portfolio for a long time already.

Position: Sale of one or major call contracts that do not exceed the investor's total number of shares in their portfolio.

Bias: Boredom

Risk: Normal downside prospect of owning a stock, as well as the cost of opportunity the stock should go above the price of call strike.

Potential for profit: Premium charged

Prices for break-even: strike price + premium charged

Registered accounts: Simple margin, including self-managed investment accounts

Key insights: Covered calls are a simple tool for investors who feel that a stock is likely to stall or stabilise for a while and want to earn premium while they are waiting higher for the next leg. The main danger with this approach is that without you on board, the stock is taking off to the upside.

4. Straightforward approaches

If you are the type of investor that likes placing small bets and working with probabilities, vertical strategies will be right up your alley. If you trade a put at $45 and buy a put at $50 and get a premium of $2.50, your break-even is $47.50. At expiration, you want the stock to close beyond the highest strike price.

Short/long call put spread:

A bullish bet that only needs ample margin to cover the overall risk and can be changed by adjusting the gap between the strike prices.

Position: Buy one call and sell one call with the same expiration at a higher strike price, or sell/buy a put at the next lower strike price of the same expiration.

Bias: Evil

Risk: Difference between the two strike prices minus any earned premium

Potential for profit: Awarded premium

Break-even price: The closer strike price less the premium for a put spread, and the closer strike price plus any premium for a call spread.

Registered accounts: Simple margin, with additional approvals including self-directed investment accounts.

Key insights: These two approaches behave the same, with operations just slightly different. If you take one another's nearest strike rates. Usually, you'll have to wait for income to expire. If the strikes are further away, or if the stock moves in the right direction far enough away, by closing the position early, and still profit.

Broad range / short call

These are bearish bets which operate in the exact opposite of their above bullish cousins.

Additional insights: The more convenient the stock is to the price of the hit, or the higher the IV index, the greater the premium.

5. Calendars Strategies

If you think a stock is unlikely to go anywhere, spread the calendar, or spread the time, work very well. This is a technique that requires both manual supervision and closure.

It is stretching long/short calendar.

The strategy uses the assumption that, on near expiry dates, the premium decays much faster than on further days.

Position: Either selling a call or placing it at a strike price and buying a call or placing it at the same strike price with the expiry date afterward.

Odds: Neutral

Risk: the difference between the premium of the month back and the premium of the month front

Benefit potential: Back month premium minus the front-month premium

Pries break-even: Difficult to quantify given a wide range of variables

Eligible accounts: Standard margin, like self-directed investment accounts with more approvals

Key insights: This technique is very tricky because it relies on a stock that does not move and gets the timing right. When the front-month expires, you will have to close the trade manually.

3.2. Tips for Effective Use of Options Trading Strategies

The fact that options trading strategies are complicated and risky is a pervasive myth about them. However, the reality is that options are nothing more than a vehicle for various ways of gaining exposure to stocks. You see, categorising options are hard to understand very easily but knowing only a few basic features about options makes them very useful and easy to understand. Anyone can learn how to trade options with confidence.

Tip 1: Options really should be considered an extension to stocks

Have you ever been in a position, as a trader, where you weren't sure you should hold stock or let it go? Anyone who has traded before has undoubtedly faced that question before and often has options at your disposal that allow much-needed flexibility when your investment faces setbacks.

In the case of stock trading alone, you are limited to initiating bullish exposure by purchasing shares and bearing exposure through shorts. Your avenue to winning trade lies in your ability to correctly guess stock direction, whereas you can bet long or short with less overall risk and lower capital outlay with options. These added profits are just a tiny fraction of what is available when options are traded. But the main outcome here is that options are nothing more than extra options traders have to express an investment idea in their toolbox.

Tip 2: Chances can be set in your favour

Believe it or not, trading options can grant you to put the odds in your favour, meaning you can place trades where you're more likely to be profitable than 50 percent! And these are not trades that add additional risk when compared with stock trading alone.

Actually, they can reduce your risk. Both types of configurations make options much more valuable than merchandising stocks alone. For one thing, you love stacking the odds in my favour when it comes to making a trade, and in my case, Options for Beginners, you do live trades where the odds are stacked in my favour.

When you buy a stock, you need to increase the stock to profit from it. If you sell a stock short, you want the stock to go down so that you can profit. These two trades define the effects of 50 percent essentially, no real edge. So imagine that you're bullish on a stock, and now you have the ability to make money if the stock is rising, standing still or falling a small amount. This is where options can become compelling to a successful portfolio.

You're sure we can all agree that, as he makes an investment decision, Warren Buffett places the chances of success in his favour. What you might not realise is that he's one of the world's biggest users of options. When used correctly, options enable you to have many opportunities that give you an edge in trade. And let's be frank, with one edge we all want to exchange.

Tip 3: Fear and greed can mean huge profits for traders' options

When seeking attractive options trades, the adage to be "fearful when others are cautious and cautious when others are fearful" can be used.

There are periods when a stock outlook is particularly grim, and the risk-reward sets up nicely for the trader of options. Trading, in contrast to consensus, will always skew the odds in your favour. I am sure we've all seen news stories; market turmoil, etc. bounce around stocks – only to see the stock finally return to its previous level. Being able to use options during these events can provide enticing trading setups where greed and fear provide the experienced investor with a chance.

One thing you would do when these situations occur is to determine the outcomes from the get-go in all possibilities, and when things line up, it's time to strike. Being prepared to take advantage of market uncertainty is an opportunity the investor knows how to make use of. You won't always be on the leading side of the deal, but if you're constantly searching for possibilities that will place you the investor in the position that will most likely gain, in the long run, you're going to come out ahead. Investing is a long game, so turning your attention away from being the "gambler" to being the "home" will give you the advantage to be successful.

Tip 4: Options like no other tool available will improve portfolios

You are not thinking about adding lots of more risk as you think about improving a portfolio.

What you are really thinking about is the use of risk management tools and the contribution of profits to a portfolio, which is not possible with trading stocks alone. There are times when changes are warranted, and times when they are not. The trick is to be alert to the right configurations that will support your portfolio over time. If your aim in nature is steady growth, revenue-oriented, or short-term, if you make the right bets with the odds in your favour, you'll be placed for success.

The aim to always strive for is consistency when taking the decision to improve your portfolio. When a portfolio is stretched, there are opportune periods for an options investor, and there are favourable periods when a portfolio is under pressure. It is vitally important to be able to recognise those occasions with a clear mind. Just as a car mechanic is only as good as his tools allow him to be, the options trader must use the right tools to improve a portfolio at the correct time.

Effective enhancement strategies are available to trader options of any level, particularly beginners. Trades in options seldom need to be complicated to affect a portfolio, and you are going through some of your favourite strategies in Investopedia Academy's Options for Beginners course.

Tip 5: Patience is the path to benefit for trader options

There are positive businesses, poor businesses, winning businesses, and losing businesses.

There'll be good trades that turn out to be losing (and that's all right), and bad trades that turn out to be winning. The trick is to know that making good solid, sound trades is the highest chance of success. One field where stock traders and traders of options can struggle is caution – they feel the urge to transact often aggressively. I compare a cautious options trader to a hitter waiting for the perfect pitch in the ring. Those are the pitches for which you swing because the time is right, and the chances of success are high. Trading on options is no different from caution. If you don't have a game strategy and recklessly deal, you possibly will strikeout. But, if you wait to come along with the perfect setup, in the right stock – that's your slow pitch.

Most of the battle is identifying the difference between good and bad trades. Once you start focusing on smarter trading, your batting average starts to increase. There are not even the most talented batters and options traders out there; their edge comes from being excellent in concentrating their skills on certain occasional good trades.

7 Trading Options for Beginners + 3 Bonus Tips

Trading options is a convenient way to make money on stocks, and sometimes profitable. Nonetheless, if you're new to trading options, then these simple guidelines will certainly come in handy as you launch your first trades and create strategies for your options.

There are a few crucial things to consider about options trading to beginners and veterans alike before we get started.

Risk Prevention

Next, trading options are a great way to manage the risk for investors.

Investors have the option to take positions representing long-term outcomes, short-term outcomes, or neutral positions while contemplating a trading options strategy.

Versatility can be a major risk reduction factor.

Yet, risk comes with all investments.

To summarise it, it's your duty to handle risk as an investor. Trading options have been called gambling in the past, so pursuing options without a plan and understanding the basics is a bit like gambling.

It shouldn't be like this.

If you're new to the world of options trading, or you'd like to see if trading options suit your overall investment strategy well, read on for seven easy options trading tips for beginners (plus three errors to avoid).

1. There are customisable choices. Talk very flexibly.

Trading options are different from conventional trading, where you're basically trying to buy low and sell big.

Traders will benefit from the use of options by forecasting downturns, inflation, and general uncertainty, as well as upturns.

The versatile nature of options trading means traders who are new to options will have even more to consider before making a move. Get ready to look for new places and seize opportunities.

With this versatility in trading, new tactics come in for success, and new tactics contribute to new strategies. For example, the "straddling" strategy allows traders to benefit from the options by predicting the volatility of a stock.

Whether the stock spikes or falls, the straddle position will lead the trader to a win. In the world of options trading, this kind of versatile position is common but uncommon when it comes to other forms of investments.

2. Trading options May be used to reduce risk. Use Hedging Options.

Trading options provide investors with the means to limit their risks.

If you're unsure about a stock's stability, but you don't want to sell it, some options let you hedge your position. A common strategy involves buying a stock put option, which will allow you to get out at a good price, even if the stock is nose-diving.

These forms of hedging opportunities are abundant in trading options and make a compelling case for investors to dip their toes into the trading pool of options.

There are, of course, no guarantees.

Also, traders with seasoned options realise there is no such thing as full risk elimination.

3. Trading options lets you call the shots. Sale and buy the stock at a price you choosing.

Traders use smart options to use options to fine-tune their overall trading strategy. That means leveraging their hard-earned market insight.

At a certain time, with options you can buy or sell a stock at a certain price.

While most basic investment platforms allow you to set your own buy and sell stock prices, buying, selling, and exercising options can expand your profit opportunities dramatically.

When it comes to selling and buying stock, strategies such as covered calls and cash-secured puts will give you more leverage and profit potential.

Jump right to the core of successful trading options tactics and strategies.

4. Know your "Points break-even."

Any right that you buy or sell has a point of break-even.

Knowing your break-even points can norm steering clear of one of the biggest mistakes that can be avoided when dealing with options: failing to stick to your plan.

The break-even point is a fixed point (high or low) that a stock price must hit to begin making a profit for the option owner.

Break-even points must take into account both the price paid for owning the option and the commissions charged on the buy and sell trade.

Make sure you do your research and take a holistic approach when using options trading strategies. There's no downside to being prepared, but there's a lot of risk going blindly at this!

5. Do the work you are doing. Don't restrict yourself to the Map of choices.

The options scheme charts the option's own actions and pricing trends but does not always provide sufficient insight into the conduct of the underlying asset — the stock.

It is necessary to understand a stock to the best of your ability before you buy or sell any related options.

My advice would be this: look out for the option charts, but don't forget your stock charts analysis.

Recall what options trading are, at its most basic level: stock positions. There is no option without that underlying asset.

6. If Selling Options Go with the Flow. Trend Line on the Bottom

There's an old adage about investing: "Trend is your buddy."

It is very important that you do not try to guess where you think a sinking stock will be plateauing or where a rising stock will level off when assessing the value of the underlying stocks.

Sorry but you're just never going to be right.

If you think you can measure the odds with (educated) guesses, you are truly gambling.

Still think patterns are going to continue.

One hundred percent of the time, you're not going to be right — that's just how trading works.

But more than once, you're going to be right, and if you've got a solid investment strategy you need to turn it into a profit.

7. Know the Plan to Escape. Always have a strategy for the exit.

When it comes to trading options – just like stock trading – leave your emotions at the door. No one is a robot, but the company is trading.

Things to remember: Have a schedule, adhere to the plan, and implement the plan.

This is to have a clearly defined exit strategy. Exit strategies aren't only effective when things go-ahead for the worse.

Also, it's important to learn when to leave, even when things go the way you planned.

To put it another way, don't hold on to south going trades if you're attached. And don't linger on trades which have hit their price targets out of greed already.

Do you choose to roll the dice on a one-off success or keep your stress levels down and produce stable revenues?

You wonder whomever you'd choose one. Don't distance yourself from the program.

Making the right judgment when trading options is crucial, but perhaps it is even more important to understand which mistakes to avoid.

A win is always the target, but the best we can do sometimes is simply not to lose. And then there are three options that trade errors to avoid at all costs.

Bonus Tips: 3 Errors Trading Beginners Options to Stop

1. Hold a Head Degree. Don't fall victim to the illusion of sunk costs.

Losses, in general, are a very real aspect of trading and selling options.

That's part of why a successful approach aims at reducing risk at each turn.

Nonetheless, the main idea here is to stop falling victim to sunk cost syndrome.

Sunk cost syndrome happens when someone takes a financial hit, so they go further into the hole in an attempt to save their investment instead of breaking off their engagement.

In the world of professional gamblers, sunk cost syndrome comes up quite a bit. Rationally, we all know there are statistical myths to winning "streaks."

Yet when someone has poured too much money into a table game or a slot machine, they sometimes believe that gambling, even more, is the only way to win back their money.

That is pretty dangerous, and it goes without saying.

Don't double down when selling options to try to recoup capital in a volatile environment.

Stick to the plan and keep your head straight. Doubling up on a losing role simply means the losses would be twice as high.

2. Stay Active. Do not Rely on Hope.

Hope isn't a strategy. Good karma, good intention, and a positive outlook are great qualities to have, but none of these alone will drive a successful trading strategy for options.

Trust in facts, trends, and rely on your experience.

Duplicate successes and look for losses.

Do your research, and take your time.

The same sense that comes from rolling the dice is to hope for the best outcome, and gambling has no place in the world of options trading.

3. Hold Head Above Snow. Don't just go Bankrupt!

It may seem like front-slipping simple advice, but don't clear up trading options for your accounts only because there's the opportunity to turn a profit.

Going broke trading options means that a few important stuffs went wrong.

If you fail to integrate exit plans into your overall investment strategies, you risk leaving too much capital in an unsustainable position.

It also leaves you vulnerable to the sunken cost syndrome, or other emotion-based choices that may disrupt your plan.

Need more tips on clichés?

Wait for the unexpected.

Understand that risk is greater than the mere location of your options and even greater than the risk associated with the underlying asset (the stock).

Deploy a contingency plan. Don't let an unexpected incident wipe your account off.

CHAPTER 4: BECOME A GOOD OPTIONS TRADER

Options are one of the most flexible financial-market instruments. Versatility influences the trader's position to increase returns. Often, they allow the consumer to manage the risk by using them to hedge or to make a profit from the market's upside/downside and sideways movements.

Trading options carries a considerable risk of loss and it has a very speculative nature, but it also has many benefits. Not everybody will become a good options trader.

Same as for other job positions, a good options trader requires a certain set of skills, personality style and attitude.

4.1 Best Ways to Master the Options Trading

1. Be Capable of Managing Risk

Options are high-risk instruments, and it is crucial for traders to understand: how much risk they have to face? What is the trade's maximum downside? What is the implicit or explicit position regarding volatility?

How much of my money is earmarked for commerce? These are some of the questions that traders should always keep in mind.

Traders must also take appropriate risk-control steps. Especially if you are a short-term options trader, you can frequently find yourself in loss-making trades. For example, if you hold a position and something changes overnight due to adverse news, your bet could go bad. You always must be able to mitigate the risk of your positions. Some traders do this by reducing their trade size and diversifying their portfolio into several different trades, so that not all their eggs are in the same basket.

An options trader must be an outstanding money manager. They need to make wise use of their capital. No matter what's approach that you will follow, you cannot forget to take in consideration risk management and money management.

2. Be Nice on Numbers

You are always dealing with numbers whilst trading in options. What does volatility imply? Is that an in the money or an out of the money option? Why is Market Break-even? Those are the questions an option trader always has to be able to answer. They also apply to Greek options, such as delta, gamma and theta of their trades in options. A trader would like to ask, for example, if his trade is short gamma.1

3. Discipline Yourself

Options traders have to practice discipline in order to become successful. That implies to do extensive research, identify opportunities, create the right trade, shape and stick to a plan, set goals and develop an exit strategy. Following the crowd is one simple example of deviating from the discipline. Never trust an opinion unless you do your own research. You can't skip the homework and blame your losses on others. You must instead formulate an independent trading strategy that works in order to make it a successful options strategy.

While scholar education, in the form of higher degrees, can be associated with the elite traders, it is not necessarily the case for everyone. But you have to be business educated. It takes time for good traders to learn the basics, study the market (various scenarios and specific trends) and know anything, and more, about how the business works. Normally, they're not novices, who took a three-hour trading seminar on "How to get rich fast with trading", but those who take the time to learn from the market.

4. Patient

Patience is one attribute that makes great a trader. Patient investors are willing to wait until the market provides the right opportunity instead of trying to make a big win on any market move.

Often you will see traders sitting lazily watching the market, waiting for the perfect time to enter or exit a company. It's not the case for hobby traders: they are nervous, unable to control their emotions and entering and leaving trades very fast.

5. Create A Style of Trade

Every trader has a different personality and should follow a trading style that fits his/her characteristics. Some traders might be good at day trading, where they buy and sell options to make small profits many times during the day, others may be more pleased with position trading, where trading strategies are built to take advantage of unique opportunities, such as time decline and volatilities and some others may find swing trading more relaxing, where traders make bets on price movement over periods of five to 30 days.

6. Tell What's New

Based on this information, it is important for traders to be able to understand the news, distinguish speculation from fact and make appropriate decisions. You'll find several traders willing to bring their money into an option with promising news, and they'll move on to the next one the day after. That distracts them from recognizing bigger market trends. Most of the successful traders will be frank with them and propose personal choices rather than simply going through the latest news.

7. Be A Successful Apprentice

The Chicago Board of Trade (CBOT) estimated that 90 percent of traders' options were lost. Successful traders are able to learn from their losses and apply what they know in their trading strategies, that makes the difference. Elite traders practice and practice before they know the lessons behind the trade, understand the economies behind the market and see the actions of it as it is.

Financial markets are constantly changing and evolving; you need to have a good understanding of what's going on and how it works. By being an active learner, you're not only going to be successful at your current trading strategies, you're also going to be able to find new opportunities that others do not see.

8. Be Smooth

You can't put a claim on the market, but you have to go with it or quit it if you don't like it. You have to accept losses that will happen, and that you will eventually lose money at some point. Acceptance, rather than market battle, is crucial to comprehension, consistency and ultimately to succeed.

9. Plan Your Company

An options trader who plans to succeed is more likely to achieve his goals than one who works on instinct and feelings.

You're going to place random trades if you don't have a strategy and, eventually, you're going to be directionless. If you have a schedule, on the other hand, you're more likely to stick to that. You'll be sure what your goals are and how you're planning to achieve them. You'll also be able to cover your expenses. You will see how this strategy worked (or didn't work) for you. All these steps are necessary for a strong trading strategy to grow.

10. Keep Records

Most active options traders keep track of their moves diligently. Keeping proper trading records is an important habit that will help you avoid costly decision making. Furthermore, the past of your sales reports provides a wealth of information to help you improve your chances of success.

Master One strategy, traders, before learning others

Once you start something new, the pull is to try to learn as much as possible in the shortest amount of time. It's human nature; when we like something, we want to overdo it a little. Trade is no different. You're excited and eager to know, so you're buying lots of trading books, reading lots of strategic articles and trying to pick out a few items from each book/article/video, putting them together into your own special trading genius mix. After all, you're learning something, it seems like the right thing to do, but it's long, costly and does not automatically produce positive results.

Below, you'll find out why you should concentrate on only learning one technique at a time when starting out and how to move through all the information, so you don't waste your time learning things that won't necessarily help you.

Avoiding Information Overload

There are so many information when you enter a sector that it may seem like you need to learn all of them. What you should be concentrating on, depends on what you want: just want to sound smart? Or want to make some money?

Almost all active traders use only a few metrics of the technical analysis to create a strategy. Such tools can include a MACD chart, moving average, Fibonacci retracing chart or trend line. If you want to sound smart, you need to know something, but that's not going to help you make money. As just mentioned, if you just need one or two tools to build a effective plan, why do you need to know about hundreds of different tools for technical analysis?

Why Just One Trading Strategy?

Most effective traders use only one strategy or two.

A strategy is a set of specific conditions outlining when you will enter and exit the market. It allows you to critically view trading opportunities and see how past trading have been played out earlier.

Although past performances are not always indicative of future results, they give you a basis for assessing whether your plan will produce a profit or not.

Since markets range (move sideways) or trend (move up or down for continuous periods) only one strategy is neded that works in both ways; alternatively, you can adopt one strategy for each market type. There's little need to try and use a lot of strategies. Become very good at one, and it will serve you a lot better than poorly interchange a whole host of strategies.

That's the real reason for using only one technique when you start. The only way to get something right is to get it done, in all sorts of market conditions over and over again. Practicing a technique in a demo account for one month will do a lot more for you to learn something than trying to absorb as much information as you can. The practice is really going to help you to develop a system that will let you make money, the same way as books make you look smart. And we all know that there is a difference between know something and actually being able to do something.

You will know your strategy inside and outside because you have practice and study it a lot. If you do that, you're going to avoid many problems that many traders face.

You're not going to hesitate to make a trade (no hesitation about trading), and you're going to get in and out at the right times (no massive losses or being stressed because you don't know what to do).

Become a one-way export. Until you're not able to execute a plan for about six months in a row (almost flawlessly, because none of us is perfect) don't even consider learning something new.

One Approach and Stick to That

Being an expert at one strategy that makes money is far better than knowing tons of procedures that you don't know how to execute and earn money from.

Final Word on a Trading Strategy

Read the basics of the market you want to trade in, before you start your journey, these include order types, capital requirements, legal and tax details, position-sizing and market hours. Then find one or two outlets that provide a timeline, business and time of day strategies that you want to trade. Open a demo account and try one of the techniques to practice. Stick with it and don't get distracted by all the other out-there stuff.

You'll probably lose money at first, no matter the plan you choose to use. Trading is a tough market and that's why you need to become a master at executing that one strategy.

With practice, you're going to get better at implementing your strategy and hopefully start seeing some positive results — this could take months. Stick to it and turn the capital into a real trading one, when you have some months of successful demo practice under your belt, with that approach. Continue to focus on that specific method, and don't add to your arsenal any more strategies until you are successful in a real money account for several months.

4.2 Tips to Become a Pro Options Trader

Binary options trading provides an excellent way for investors to make profits while not being under much pressure at the same time.

What makes it so famous is the simplicity of it. It may seem easy to have different choices choosing between two possible outcomes, but you should not forget that there is always some degree of risk involved.

If you're an inexperienced trader looking to step up his business efforts, we'll help you out and give you some tips on how to become a professional one!

1. Select a Broker

The most obvious thing we should start with - find a broker. As simple as it seems, it can be more difficult to find a broker that is ideal for you than it may seems at first glance.

There are tons of different brokers out there, offering their services to investors, and although they all operate on the same principles, there are a few different things that you need to look at.

You need to know clearly what you are trying to achieve with your goals, what you are planning to do and how much money you are willing to deposit.

With these things in mind, you can go around and take a look at the ratings of binary brokers to find the best one for you. Make sure to read what the users say to make sure you don't choose a scam broker.

2. Allow the most of Demo Accounts

Not all binary brokers, but most of them, offer access to a demo account for consumers. Having no experience in the field means you can seriously benefit from it.

You can look around and see what the trading platform has to offer, play around, make some asset forecasts and see how the market is moving.

This is important for new traders, they will gain the trust and experience they need, without risking their money.

3. Say what you do at home

You need to have some information about the theory before you start putting it into action.

You will find several useful guides and videos on internet, which will teach you the basics of binary trading and train you for the real world of trade.

4. Set Real goals and limits

Yeah, doubling your money in one click is good, but you can't do that all the time. Even if lady luck is on your side, you have to plan and carry out some diligent execution.

The most important thing you can do is to set a realistic target. You don't just want to risk it all and take huge gambles. Since there are serious risks involved, you need to be careful on how much you're depositing. Be aware of the money you deposit, and never use more than you can afford to lose.

5. Choose what you find best to work with

Brokers selling binary options offer various assets with which investors can trade. The four most common groups are: currencies, indices, commodities and inventories.

Commonly, the inexperienced trader is familiar with currencies and commodities. In fact, if you're a beginner, starting your trading efforts with those two assets is the right way to go, since they are the easiest to predict.

6. Go at Your Own Pace

You may be fooled into thinking you can jump straight away and be on the same level as experienced traders. As simple as it looks, though, binary trading can still be risky and challenging.

Set your own pace, and don't hurry. While practicing, you'll learn more and more about the market, and you'll gain the confidence and experience you need to start trading on larger amounts and less volatile assets, that will bring more benefits.

7. Do some tests

You may only have two options to choose from, but that means the probability of a win is 50:50. If you want to learn how things work, by investing small amounts of money, like several dollars, you can conduct your own test on different assets. Thanks to this, you'll learn more about the market and the changes that can happen. Being a binary options trader, even for novices, can be a very profitable thing.

But to achieve your goals, you need to get going somewhere and start on solid foundations.

CHAPTER 5: MAKE A HUGE INCOME FROM INVESTING IN OPTIONS TRADING AND OTHER ASSETS

Wealth investing is the practice of designing a portfolio of diversified investments, in order to achieve a living on passive income. This can include real estate, shares, mutual funds and bonds. It is important to observe which types of assets might be of the greatest value to someone who wanted to follow an income investment philosophy and understand the most common dangers that can affect a portfolio of income investors.

5.1 10 STEPS TO SUCCESSFUL INCOME INVESTING FOR BEGINNERS

Do you need to build a cash-generating portfolio? Are you more concerned with paying your bills and having enough income than growing richer? If so, consider using an old investment technique, investing in sales.

Until the great twenty-year bull market, everybody was led to assume that the only decent investment was one you purchased for $10, and sold for $20. Although income investment has gone out of style with the general public, this discipline is still practiced quietly across the mahogany-panelled offices of the world's most respected wealth management firms.

1. Defined Wealth Investing

A portfolio of assets such as stocks, bonds, mutual funds and real estate, which will generate the highest potential annual income at the lowest risk possible, is the art of good income investing. Most of this money is paid out to the investor so they can use it to buy clothes, pay bills and take vacations, or whatever else they want to do in their lives.

2. How the 20th-century social unrest gave birth to investment in income

Despite some nostalgia for the nineteenth and early twentieth, society was pretty chaotic. The chaos wasn't due to the lack of instant news, video chats, music-on-demand, 24-hour stores and vehicles that could travel over ten miles per gallon.

If you were Jewish or Irish, you would not be hired by most corporations, you were given electroshock therapy if you were gay or lesbian, black men and women were coping with the persistent threat of mob lynching and rape.

If you were a woman, you could not get a job doing anything more than typing, for which you'd be paid a fraction of the amount for similar work offered to a male.

Add to all of this that no social security or employer pension plans existed, resulting in miserable poverty among most elderly people.

What all this have to do with earnings investment? These are the conditions that caused income investment to rise, when you are peeling back the layers, and it's not hard to understand how.

Income Investment Increase

The decent-paying labour markets were effectively closed for everyone except for the well-connected white men. One important exception: if you owned stocks and bonds from companies like Coca-Cola or PepsiCo, there was no idea of such investments whether you were black, white, male, female, young, old, smart, working, pretty, small, tall, big, fat, it didn't matter.

Throughout the year, you have been sent dividends and interest depending on the overall amount of your investment and how well the company has performed. That's why it was a quasi-ironclad rule that you saved until you had enough money, and the only appropriate investment philosophy was to invest in cash.

The thought of selling stocks would have been an anathema (and literally pointless, as commissions in the 1950s could take you as high as $200 to $300 per trade — the equivalent of $2,000 to $3,000 in 2020).

3. The portfolio of the Widow bursts onto the scene

Essentially, these social realities meant that women were considered, by the society, vulnerable without a man. Up until the 1980s, you will still hear people talking about an income-investing portfolio as a "widow's portfolio."

That was because it was a routine task for officers, in the community banks' trust department, to take the life insurance money that a widow got after the death of her husband and put together a list of stocks, bonds and other properties.

Such investments will create enough monthly income for her to pay the bills, keep the house and raise the kids without having a breadwinner. In other words, her goal was not to become wealthy but to do everything possible to maintain a certain level of income to maintain the family.

Today, we are living in a world where women are as likely to get a job as men, potentially even earning more money. Nevertheless, if your husband died in the 1950s, you had almost no chance of substituting your family for the full benefit of his income.

That is why investment in income was such an important practice that every trust officer, bank employee, and stockbroker needed to understand it.

AT&T stocks are no longer referred to as "a widow's stock" by anyone, which should have been his second name a generation or two ago.

Today, with pension systems going the dinosaur's way, and 401(k) balances wildly fluctuating, plaguing most of the nation's working class, there has been a resurgence of interest in income investment.

4. How Much Cash would you expect from a Portfolio of Income Investments?

If you've never desired to run out of money, the rule of thumb, in income investment, is that you should take no more than 4 percent of your income balance out each year. This is commonly referred to as the 4 percent law on Wall Street. That is because if the economy collapses, 5 percent of academic work has been shown to cause you to run out of money in as early as 20 years, while 3 percent have not.

Simply put, if you manage to save $350,000 by retirement at age 65 (which would only take $146 a month from the time you were 25 years old and gain 7% a year), you would be able to make $14,000 annual withdrawals, without ever running out of money. This works against a self-made pension fund of about $1,166 a month before tax.

Strategy for Multiple Earnings

If you are a typical retired worker, you can earn Social Security benefits of up to $1,500 a month in 2020. A spouse will add her earning social security benefits, getting to an average of about $2,500; add $1,166 a month from a pension fund withdrawal, and you'll get a nice $3,666 a month.

At the time of your retirement, you will own your own house and have very little debt, so you should be able to meet your basic needs in the absence of any major medical emergencies. Through doing some part-time work, you might potentially add another $500 to $600 a month to your monthly income.

You can change your withdrawal rate if you're willing to risk running out of money sooner. Unless you doubled the withdrawal rate to 8 percent and your investment gained 6 percent with an inflation of 3 percent, you will actually lose 5 percent of the account value, in real terms, annually.

That would be worse if the market collapsed, and when stocks and bonds will be small, you will be forced to sell shares. However, within 20 years, you'd only be able to withdraw $500 to $600 a month (around $300 to $400 in dollars in 2020).

5. Which Asset Forms Can You Keep for your Income Portfolio?

When you build up your portfolio of income investments, you will have three major "buckets" of potential assets. Including:

Dividend-paying options: These are valuable for both common and preferred stocks. Companies paying dividends, pay shareholders a portion of their annual income, depending on the number of shares they own. Aim to pick companies with healthy dividend pay-out ratios, which mean they are distributing 40 to 50 percent of their annual income and reinvesting the rest back into the company for growth. For some time, a dividend yield of 4 to 6 percent has generally been considered fine.

Bonds: When it comes to bonds, you have a lot of options. You may own government bonds, agency bonds, municipal bonds or other savings bonds. Whether you are buying corporate or municipal bonds, depends on your personal equivalent taxable return, you shouldn't buy the one with longer maturities than 5 to 8 years, because you face the risk of duration, the chance of wildly fluctuating bonds, like stocks in response to Federal Reserve-controlled interest rate shifts.

Real Estate: Rental properties may be held directly or invested in land investment trusts (REITs). Real estate has its own tax laws, and some people are more relaxed, since the property provides some protection against high inflation.

Most portfolios of income investment have a strong real estate component, since their tangible existence generates lasting value. Psychologically, this gives the necessary peace of mind during fluctuating markets in order to stick to a financial plan.

A closer look at each category will give you a better idea of appropriate portfolio investment for revenue investing.

6. What to look for in an Income Management Portfolio Dividend Stocks

You'd want dividend stocks that have multiple characteristics in your personal income investment portfolio. You would want to have a dividend payout ratio of 50 percent, or a bit less, with the rest going back to the business of the company for future growth.

If a company pays too much of its income, it can harm the competitive position of the company. A dividend profit of 2 to 6 percent is a good payout. That means that if a company has a stock price of $30, it will pay cash dividends between $0.60 and $1.80 per share per year.

For the past three years, that company should have produced at least positive earnings with no losses. Income investment is about preserving and delivering revenue, not hitting hard to hit the ball, with risky stock picks, out of the park.

History of the business, and financial performance

Preferred is a proven track record of (slowly) increasing dividends. If management is helpful to shareholders, it would be more eager to return excess cash to the stockholders than in expanding the empire, especially in mature businesses with little space for growth.

Other factors are the return on equity of a company (ROE — after-tax income relative to shareholder equity), and its debt-to-equity ratio. This last one is determined by dividing the equity of the shareholder by the amount of total debt that a corporation has, which shows its ability to pay its obligations.

If a company, with a reasonable debt-to-equity ratio (for its industry), will earn high returns on equity, it typically has a better financial model than the average, for income investors. In a recession, this can provide a bigger buffer and help to keep dividend controls going.

7. What Percentage Your Income Investment Portfolio to Consider?

What percentage of your portfolio of income investments should be divided among those asset classes (stocks, bonds, real estate, etc.)? The answer is: it is about your personal choices, preferences, tolerance of risks and whether or not you can tolerate a lot of volatility. Asset allocation is a personal choice.

The simplest allocation to investing income would be:

1/3 of assets in dividend-paying stocks which meet the criteria previously set

1/3 of assets in bonds or bond funds which meet the criteria previously stated

You could use the portion of your portfolio as a 50 percent down payment and borrow the rest to double own the property.

A look in detail at the numbers

What would a real portfolio look like in that allocation? Let's take a glance at a worker who retires with $350,00 (again), that will only take $146 a month between the ages of 25 and 65 at 7 percent. To keep the numbers simple, round the increment to the nearest $5:

Stocks: $108,335 invested in high-quality, 4.5 percent dividend, stocks. Annual salary expected: $4,875

Bonds: $108,335 invested in bonds of high quality, with an average yield of 4.5%. Annual salary expected: $4,875

Real Estate: $108,335 used as 50 percent equity combined with another $108,335 borrowed from the bank to buy a total property of $216,670. The estimated annual income is $15,100, after expenditures, repairs, taxes and vacancies.

Grand Total Income Pre-tax: $24,850 in cash. However, you should only take out 4 percent of the $350,000, or $14,000, for sustainable income capital, so you would leave $10,850 in your portfolio of income investors (an accounting professional should be consulted for tax consequences).

8. Bonds in an Income Portfolio

Bonds are often regarded as the cornerstone of income investment, since they typically fluctuate far less than stocks. You lend money to the company or government that issues it, with a bond. You own a slice of the company with one stock. The potential benefit from bonds is much more limited; however, you have a better chance of recovering your investment in the event of bankruptcy. This is not to say that bonds are riskless. In addition, bonds offer income investors a specific set of risks. Your choices include bonds like municipal bonds that offer tax benefits. Bond funds, which are a portfolio of bonds, could be a better option, with various investors pooling capital, like a mutual fund.

Bond Features to Prevent

One of the greatest risks is something that's called bond length. Generally, you shouldn't buy bonds that mature in more than 5-8 years, when you put together an income investment portfolio, because they can lose a lot of value, if the interest rates shift quickly.

You should also probably avoid foreign bonds because they pose some real risks when you grasp the fluctuating monetary market.

If you're trying to figure out the amount your portfolio should have in bonds, you should follow the age-old rule, which is your age, according to Burton Malkiel, A Random Walk Down Wall Street's famous author and beloved Ivy League instructor. If you are 30, then you should have 30 percent of your investments in bonds. If you're 60, then it should be 60 percent.

9. Why real estate will help double the rate of withdrawal

If you know what you're doing, real estate can be a huge investment for those who want to produce regular income (picture payments rolling in every month). This is particularly true if you are searching for a passive income that blends into your portfolio of income investment.

Your main choice is whether to purchase a property straight away or invest through a REIT. Both have their own advantages and disadvantages, but each one them may have a position in a well-built portfolio of investments.

A Major Property Benefit

One major lead of real estate is that you can drastically increase your withdrawal rate if you are comfortable using debt, because the property itself will keep pace with inflation. Anyway, this approach is not risk-free.

You may be able to effectively double the amount of monthly income you will produce if you know your local market and have other revenue, cash savings, and reserves.

Why Don't You Go All-In?

If immovable property provides higher income returns for investment, why not just put 100 percent of your investment into land?

This question is often raised when people see that they can double the monthly cash flow they will receive when buying property instead of stocks, bonds or even triple that. Three issues related to this approach are:

- If the immovable price falls, the loss is compounded by leverage; the use of debt to fund the acquisitions of real estate.
- Real estate requires more work from litigation, repairs, taxes, insurance and more, than stocks and bonds.
- The long-term rise in stock values has always beaten real estate on an inflation-adjusted basis.

10. The position of saving in a portfolio of investment in income

Mind that saving money is different than spending money. Even if you have a widely diversified portfolio of income investment, generating loads of cash every month, it's important that you have enough money on hand, in risk-free FDIC covered bank accounts, in the event of an emergency.

The amount of cash you need will depend on your total fixed payments, your debt levels, your health and your liquidity outlook (how quickly you may need to convert assets into cash).

It cannot be exaggerated the importance of holding cash in a savings account. You can wait until you have built up enough funds to cover emergencies, health insurance and easy spending. Investing will be done only at that moment, then.

5.2. 10 OPTIONS TRADING MISTAKES TO AVOID

If you are a keen investor, you've most likely heard about bonds, stocks, ETFs or mutual funds. Options are also an asset class that has unusual advantages to stock trading or ETFs, if properly traded. They can be acquired through a brokerage account, just like other asset classes.

Options are an outstanding investment vehicle, as they maximize earnings security and have leverage.

For example, they can be used as a hedge, limiting the losses in a declining stock trade. These can also be used to speculate on the course of a stock or to bring in recurring revenue. Options generally have more trading options but have just as many risks as other classes of assets.

They come under securities known as options, which is a class of assets considered highly speculative and unpredictable. Warren Buffet defined these volatile assets as "weapons of mass destruction." Derivatives origin edit ate their prices from other objects, and options develop their prices from various securities in finance.

Knowing how to trade properly in options can give you an advantage in their markets. In comparison, selling them without a good strategy can cause catastrophic losses. For example, each option trader has a limited timeframe within which to make profits from transactions he/she can trade with. Once that bus passes, the losses start growing.

Options trading are not gambling. Below are some mistakes an option trader should avoid, remaining afloat on the options market.

1. Buy Off the Money Options

Out of the money, OTM, options are usually cheaper than other options and are popular among traders. The thing about pricing options, or any asset pricing in that sense, is there is nothing like a free lunch.

The value of an acquired option will decline over time so that the price of the OTM call options will rise above or below the selling price, before the option expires. If this happens favorably, then you will be able to offset the purchase costs of your option.

While trading in OTM call options can bring some profits, making consistent profits off of them is not easy. If you're limited to OTM options only, you'll end up losing some of your trades consistently, particularly if you don't consider the asset volatility.

2. Leverage Exploit

Share buying is performed at the full price of them, when dealing with stocks. Options are 'options' and are, therefore, far more competitive than most stocks. They allow you to buy stocks at a fraction of their actual costs.

This can lead the majority of traders to put more money into one options trading than they should, thank to trade overleveraging. To master the leverage, an options trader must learn. Ensure your losses are limited to between 1% and 5% of your overall trading portfolio. It means that you won't lose too much if a trade goes south, and you can pick yourself up and try a different deal.

3. Does not have an Escape Strategy

A strong stock investor, when it comes to investing, needs to be very level headed. A handle on emotions will help you stay healthy by making a strategy and by sticking to it, while dealing with choices. A good strategy should have an escape route to take, even though things seem to be going your way.

The upside/downside exchange should have exit points, and all timeframes for exits should be followed. The goal here is to constantly make more profit and to keep you competitive, with fewer losses. You'll be tempted to disregard the exit point of a deal, of course, but this is when you most need self-control.

4. Eviting New Trading Approaches

Keep your ear on the table, and don't get used to just one method of trading. Options prices shift differently from their underlying stock. Be versatile and diversify your trading strategies to ensure you can apply specific trading conditions for different assets according to their preferences.

5. Trading in Commodities Which are Not Really Volatile

A liquid asset allows traders to quickly purchase it and sell it off and markets with these assets, have players active and ready. Stocks are of a more liquid nature than options. This is because stock assets aren't as different as the option assets. Illiquid options raise high trading costs, so choose liquid ones.

6. Keep Abreast of Market Events

When the market condition is quiet, some traders buy options and make some money, as the trade stays discreet. If you don't check if there are any movements due during the time frame of the trading, like an earnings release, the market conditions could suddenly change and increase the volatility of the asset. So, tracking the options' economic calendar and developing a trading plan around them is important.

7. Running Down Waterfalls

While making enormous gains can be exciting, are the smaller incremental improvements that keep you through. Home runs during real-time trading are not easy to spot. On the other hand, making small, regular wins will create your wealth. Losing a home-run trade could cost you further capital gains, making the losses recovering very difficult.

8. Decide the Wrong Size of a Transaction

Let the sizes of your preference suit you're trading expertise. Do not risk taking too much investments into your portfolio. Allow time and practice to work out what's the best size for your portfolio to exchange.

9. Don't Believe in Yourself

Know more about options trading and it'll pay off by helping you create better opportunities for trading.

Tip: Buy your cash options so you can live debt-free or, with online lenders, take some loans up to $5000. If you trade with money, you're only at risk of losing the amount of capital you've invested. Make sure the money is yours and not credit, especially if you're a new trader. Borrowed money has interest charges, and that will eat up most of your gains or make your losses even worse. When you open long position trades regularly, you won't have to worry about being in debt either.

10. Not Getting A Coach/ Mentor

Have a trading partner who will hold you responsible for your strategy, will help you stay on the right side of the trading line. A partner in accountability may be a relative, a sibling or a spouse who will monitor your progress and keep you in charge.

The last word

Trading in options is an excellent way to achieve wealth, but only if it is played by market rules. Those financial assets will diversify your trading portfolio, if they are well implemented. New traders, in options trading, should first begin with paper trading.

The trading paper will give you a hands-on experience of what's needed while trading options. Any trader will make some trading mistakes at some point. If you do that, then you should adapt and try again. Even better, try to avoid making the mistakes mentioned above, and you'll find it easier to find your flow in trading and to create the income you want.

5.3. How to Make Your Investments Grow

You'll need to make the good old way of making your money, work for that. Nonetheless, you can get an advantage from knowing how to make money. There are four major ways to make money, and they might help you to shape a fortune.

Selling Time Is Money Made.

Source of income considered the most significant by the lower or middle classes. This is the amount of money you get to sell your time, or investment, to an employer. These are also portrayed as wages, or salaries. Often you will hear well-meaning parents telling their children to find a " job" that may have benefits.

The cost that you get for your time depends on how unique and important your skills are to society. For example, a talented brain surgeon will charge millions of euros/dollars per year because there are simply not many women/men who can do the job. Someone who shoves carts at a discount retailer receives less, not because they are less essential as an individual, but because practically anyone in good health can do that!

You need to invest in yourself and work longer hours, or a combination of the two, to earn more money. That form of compensation is the most tyrannical way to make a living because you only produce money while you are actively employed. A talented lawyer can earn millions of dollars a year, but if he doesn't work, he can't keep on living off legal fees.

The Income of Interest on Cash Lent

This kind of income comes from money lenders, who pay you to "rent" your capital (the word capital refers to funds that you have set aside for investment purposes (you'll hear it a lot on Wall Street). For example, when you buy a deposit certificate at a bank, you lend money to the bank in return for a fixed yield rate, usually a few percentage points per year. The bank takes from you the money that it "owes" and lends it out at a higher rate, pocketing the difference. (Therefore, the yield curve is so critical for those of you who are interested).

It's the short-term and long-term tariff partnership. The steeper the developed ideas, the more money your bank will makes from it on your certificate of deposit or savings account.

Benefit Dividend from Assets Held

That is your share of a company's profits, in which you made an investment. If you own 60% of a stand and the company has revenue of $1,200 with costs of $600 and residual income of $600, your share of those profits would be $260 (because your possession of 60% of the stock is entitled to receive 60% of the benefit). The amount that will be paid out to you is called your earnings "break". Good funding is one in which the company earns more year after year, and send to you regularly increasing amount of cash.

Similarly, like interest income, the essence of the income from dividends is that your money goes out and works for you. However, there are certain types of labor that can be included in this group. A salesman who receives commissions with little or no work on recurring orders is, in essence, running a business.

A dividend income example: My grandmother also owns a few rental properties. She buys real estate and then rent them out, someone will pay to live in her houses. In these situations, her rental business generates income equal to the total rent she receives minus any expenses, such as repairs and property upgrades.

Income Capital Gains

This form of revenue is created by purchasing an investment, or asset, at one price and selling it at another, higher, price, leading on making a profit. Going back to our lemonade stand, for example, the $3,000 difference will reflect your capital gain if you purchased your 60 percent stake in the business for $3,000 and sold it for $6,000. In recent years, many Americans have found their living standards artificially inflated during the housing boom, because the capital gains, that resulted from the increase in the value of their homes, were a source of income they believed would continue indefinitely. Go back to our ambitious grandmother: If she were to sell one of the rental house she purchased for $90,000, to a buyer who was willing to pay $140,000, then the difference of $50,000 reflects her capital gain.

There are several explanations, including:

Money earned to sell your time (salary and salaries) is also taxed at much higher levels than other income forms. The reality is, if you can make $6,000 in dividend income, you're likely to pay only $850 in taxes, while if you were a self-employed plumber who went out and earned $6,000 through hard work, you 'd probably end up paying more than $3,000 after federal taxes, payroll taxes and other charges.

There are just 24 hours a day. Then you can work for those many hours only. At some point, selling more of your time is physically impossible, because well, you ran out of it! As we have already mentioned, you can always increase the amount you receive by acquiring unique skills that are in high demand. There's practically no boundary on how much you can receive with interest, dividend and capital gains. When you put your money back into these outlets each year, a few decades from now, you will find yourself making millions of dollars annually.

5.4. Pick Right Option to Trade in Six Steps

Options can be used to execute a wide range of trade strategies, from easy buy-and-sell to complicated spreads with names such as butterflies and condors. Additionally, there are options on a wide range of stocks, currencies, commodities, exchange-traded funds and futures contracts.

There are often hundreds of strike prices and expiry dates available for each commodity, which can pose a challenge to the inexperienced buyer, because plenty of available options often make it difficult to identify a suitable trade option.

Near Takeaways

Options trading can be complex, especially when there may be many different ones with multiple strikes and expiration dates to choose from on the same underlying.

Hence it is important to find the right choice to suit your trading strategy to optimize market success.

There are six basic steps to determine and identify the right option, beginning with an investment target and culminating in a sale.

Define your target, evaluate the risk/reward, considerable uncertainty, anticipate events, plan a strategy and identify criteria for the options.

Finding the appropriate option

They start with the assumption that you have already defined a financial asset (such as stock, product, or ETF) that you wish to use to trade-in options. Using a stock screener, using your own analysis or using third-party testing, you might have selected the underlying. Regardless of the selection process, these are the six steps to find the right choice once you have identified the underlying asset for the trade:

- Formulate your target investment.
- Determine your return on the risk-reward.
- The volatility test.
- Identify happenings.
- Create a plan.
- Set parameters for selection.

The six steps follow a logical process of thinking, which facilitates the selection of a specific trading option. Let's breakdown what each move entails.

1. Objective Alternative

The starting point is your investment goal, when making every investment, and trading options are no different. Which goal do you want to achieve with your trade option? Is it speculating on a bullish view, or on a bearish one, of the underlying asset? Or is it hedging potential downside exposure to a stock you have a significant position in?

Are you putting the selling option premium on the trade to earn income? Is the tactic part of a covered call on a current stock stake, for example, or are you writing put on a stock you want to own? Use income-generating options are a vastly different approach from purchasing speculative, or hedging, options.

Your first move is to determine what the purpose of the trade is, as it forms the basis for the subsequent steps.

2. Risk / Price

The next step is to decide your payoff for risk-reward, which will depend on your risk tolerance, or risk appetite. If you're a cautious investor, or trader, then risky strategies like writing puts, or buying a large amount of money-deep (OTM) options, cannot be right for you.

Each strategy choice has a well-defined risk and reward profile, so make sure you get a detailed understanding.

3. Verify Stability

Implied volatility is one of the most critical determinants of the price of an option, so get a clear read on the ones you are considering on the level of implied volatility. Compare the degree of it with the historical volatility of the stock and the level of it in the general market, as this will be a key factor in determining your trade/strategy choice. Implied uncertainty will let you know whether other traders expect the stock to move a great deal or not. High implied volatility would drive up premiums, making writing an option more appealing, if the trader assumes that volatility won't continue to rise (which might increase the likelihood of exercising the option). High implied volatility means lower option premiums, which are ideal for purchasing options, if an investor expects the underlying stock to change enough to raise the options' value.

4. Determine Events

Events can be divided into two large categories: stock-specific and market-wide. Market-wide events are the ones that affect broad markets, such as announcements by the Federal Reserve and releases of economic data. Stock-specific events are items like reports on profits, product launches and spinoffs.

Before its actual occurrence, an event can have a significant impact on implied volatility, and when it occurs, the event can have a huge impact on the stock price. So, would you like to capitalize on the volatility spike before a key event, or would you rather sit on the side-lines before things settle?

Identifying events that could have an effect on the underlying asset, will help you assess the correct time period and expiry date for your options trade.

5. Develop a Strategy

You are now aware of your investment objective, target risk-reward return, degree of implied and historical volatility, and key events that may affect the underlying asset, based on the analysis conducted in the previous steps. Moving through the four steps helps you identifying a specific strategic option much easier.

Let's assume you're a cautious investor with a large stock portfolio, for example, and want to gain premium income before businesses start publishing their quarterly earnings, in a few months. Therefore, you may opt for a covered call writing strategy, that involves making calls to some, or all, of the stocks in your portfolio.

Another example, if you're an aggressive investor who likes long shots and is firmly convinced that within six months the markets will have a big decline, you might decide to buy major stock indices.

6. Place Parameters

Now that you have determined the specific option strategy that you wish to implement, all that's left is to set options parameters such as expiration dates, strike prices, and deltas options. For example, you might want to buy a call with the longest expiration data possible but at the lowest possible cost, in this case an out-of-the-money call may be acceptable. Equally, you could choose an in-the-money option if you want a call with a high delta.

Examples Through these steps

Here are two hypothetical examples, where different types of traders use the six steps.

Say a conservative investor holds 1,000 McDonald's (MCD) shares and is concerned about the possibility of a 5 percent + stock decline over the coming months. The buyer doesn't want the stock to be sold but wants to protect himself from a potential decline:

Objective: Hedge downside risk in current holdings of McDonald (1,000 shares); stock (MCD) trading at $161.48;

Risk / Reward: As long as it is quantifiable, the investor does not mind a little risk, but is loath to take on unlimited risk.

Volatility: ITM put options implied volatility ($165 strike price) is 17.38 percent for one-month puts and 16.4 percent for three-month puts. Market volatility is 13.08 percent, as calculated by the CBOE Volatility Index (VIX).

Events: The investor wants a hedge going beyond the Earnings report by McDonald's. In just over two months, earnings are out, meaning the options will stretch out for about three months.

Strategy: Purchasing puts, hedging the chance of the underlying stock declining.

Option Parameters: $165-strike-price puts are available at $7.15 for three months.

Since the investor needs to protect past earnings from the stock position, they are buying the $165 puts for three months. The total cost of the position put to hedge 1,000 MCD shares is $7,150 ($7.15 x 100 per contract x 10 contracts). The expense is excluding commissions.

The buyer is hedged if the stock drops, as the gain on the put option would possibly cover the stock loss.

If the stock stays flat and trades unchanged at $161.48, very soon before the puts expire, edit would have an intrinsic value of $3.52 ($165 - $161.48), which means the buyer will recoup around $3,520 of the amount invested in the puts, by selling the puts to close the bet. If the stock price rises above $165, the buyer benefits from the 1,000-share value increase but forfeits the $7,150 payable on the options. Now presume that an enthusiastic investor is optimistic about Bank of America's (BAC) prospects and has $1,000 to execute a trading options strategy:

Goal: Purchase risky Bank of America calls. The stock is $30.55 in trade.

Risk / Reward: The investor doesn't mind losing the entire $1,000 investment, but needs to get as many possibilities as possible to maximize potential profit.

Volatility: The implied volatility on OTM call options ($32 strike price) is 16.9% for one-month calls and 20.04% for four-month calls. The CBOE Volatility Index (VIX) calculated market volatility is 13.08 percent.

Events: Zero, the organization already had results, and it'll be a couple of months before the next report of results. The investor is not currently concerned with earnings, but expects that the stock market will grow over the next few months, and assumes that this stock will do especially well.

Strategy: Purchase calls from OTM to gamble on stock price spikes.

Choice Parameters: $32 calls to BAC for four months are available at $0.84, and $33 calls are provided at $0.52 for four months.

Since the buyer wants to buy as many cheap calls as possible, they're going for the $33 calls for four months. With the exception of commissions, 19 contracts are acquired, at $0.52 each, for a $988 cash outlay (19 x $0.52 x 100 = $988), plus commission.

In theory, the cumulative gain is infinite. If a global banking company arrives and agrees to buy Bank of America in the next few months for $40, the $33 calls would be worth at least $7 each, and the option position would be worth $13,300 each. The point of break-even on trade is the $33 + $0.52, or $33.52.

Note that the $33 strike price is 8 percent higher than the current price of the stock. The investor must be confident that in the next four months, the price can rise by at least 8 percent. If the price at expiry doesn't surpass the $33 strike price, the investor will lose the $988.

The Bottom Line

While the wide range of strike prices and expiry dates can make it difficult to zero on a particular option for a novice investor, the six steps outlined here follow a logical thinking process, that can help in choosing a trade option. Set your target, evaluate the risk/reward, look at uncertainty, consider events, prepare your approach, and identify criteria for your options.

CONCLUSION

There are many different ways to invest and many different financial instruments can be used for investment, and trade purposes. Like all types of trading, trading options have unique characteristics and are somewhat more complicated than many alternatives, as we have described. However, the basic concept is quite similar to any other investment firm; the goal is to make money from the purchase and sale of financial instruments.

While contract options are one of the more complex financial instruments, the principle of investing and trading them is, of course, to make money. Trading options offer many different ways to profit from a range of price movements of assets and securities. While they aren't effortless, compared to merely buying stocks, the potential rewards can make learning how to make trade options worthwhile.

Usually, use is not so difficult. Finding a broker good enough for binary options and providing trading on a trial account.

To become an options trader, you need to understand their mechanism. How different market dynamics influence their prices. Whatever options you use to reap form any market conditions. Even sluggish markets can make money. If you want to become an options trader, there's plenty to learn. It's quantitative and gives you unemotional trading power.

Many strategies limit risk and maximize return. Traders must learn how to optimize the flexibility and power options offered.

Wealth investment is the practice of designing a portfolio of diversified investments to achieve passive income. Like real estate, securities, mutual funds and bonds. It is essential to consider which asset types could be of the most significant value to someone who wanted to follow an income investment philosophy, and understand the most common dangers that can affect an income investor portfolio.